MEETING JESUS
IN THE NEW TESTAMENT

MEETING JESUS
IN THE NEW TESTAMENT

Jacqueline McMakin
and
Rhoda Nary

HarperSanFrancisco
A Division of HarperCollins*Publishers*

This book was previously published as part two in *Doorways to Christian Growth* by Jacqueline McMakin with Rhoda Nary.

FIRST EDITION

Library of Congress Cataloging-in-Publication Data
McMakin, Jacqueline.
    [Doorways to Christian growth]
    The doorways series / Jacqueline McMakin and Rhoda Nary.—1st ed.
      p. cm.
    Originally published as a single volume in 1984, under the title:
Doorways to Christian growth.
    Includes bibliographical references.
    Contents: [1] Encountering God in the Old Testament—[2] Meeting Jesus in the New Testament—[3] Journeying with the spirit—[4] Discovering your gifts, vision, and call.
    ISBN 0–06–065377–9 (v. 1).—ISBN 0–06–065378–7 (v. 2).—ISBN 0–06–065379–5 (v. 3).—ISBN 0–06–065380–9 (v. 4).
    1. Christian life—1960-   2. God—Biblical teaching.   3. Jesus Christ—Person and offices.   I. Nary, Rhoda.   II. Title.
[BV4501.2.M4358 1993]
248.4—dc20
          92–53917
          CIP

93 94 95 96 97 ❖ RRD(H) 10 9 8 7 6 5 4 3 2 1

CONTENTS

INTRODUCTION

Two thousand years ago one person lived a life so striking in its compassion, healing, and liberation that many thought he reflected the nature of God more fully than anyone else had ever done.

Today the life of every individual and the planet itself is threatened. More than ever we need to find ways to implement God's vision of wholeness and peace for ourselves and for the whole created order.

Can this person—Jesus—help us? Are his life, teachings, and empowerment of others relevant to the challenges of our personal and global existence today? These are questions no one can answer for another. We can, however, support one another as we look at the experience of Jesus and his disciples and allow ourselves to be guided, changed, and even transformed by this contact.

This course provides a setting in which to do this. In Jesus' day many people had relatively brief contacts with him, and yet often those contacts had lifelong consequences. How can we approach Jesus in ways that are decisive and life changing?

This book introduces key New Testament events and passages to show who Jesus was to the people he knew and then presents opportunity to decide who he is for us today.

The many names people have given Jesus are attempts to capture their experience of him. We chose six pairs that have had major impact on our lives and those of others:

✤ *Immanuel/God with Us*

✤ *Healer/Liberator*

✤ *Friend/Mystery*

✦ *Teacher/Guide*

✦ *Savior/Prophet*

✦ *Spirit/Presence.*

We begin by approaching Jesus as an infant, vulnerable as all newborn humans. We can be at ease in his company, laying aside our doubts, suspending our arguments (Session 1).

Next we bring our need for healing into contact with Jesus. Each of us has psychological, emotional, and physical wounds that cry out for healing—parts of our lives that are unfree. We draw a bit closer to see what this Jesus might do for us (Session 2).

Having come nearer, we are invited into a relationship with one who wants to do more than heal us. Desiring our company, he offers his friendship (Session 3).

As we open ourselves to a deeper intimacy with him, Jesus' life and words take on new meaning. His teachings—in parables, sermons, actions—take us to another level of experiencing God (Session 4).

Finally, he demonstrates the depths of his love, giving ultimate meaning to the word *Savior* (Session 5).

We move through the final events of Jesus' life and encounter the disciples' experience after his death. The power made available to them has continued for two thousand years and is available to us (Session 6).

In some ways this book is like a retreat. For some of us, it may not say anything new, but it reminds us of events and themes in the life of Jesus we already know. It provides opportunities to meditate on and to appropriate for ourselves faith experiences that were important to Jesus and his companions. You are invited to approach this course with an attitude of open-minded inquiry combined with a willingness to experience and reflect on the content.

Some contemporary thinkers raise a number of issues regarding Jesus. For example, people of other living faiths question claims that salvation can be found only through Jesus; they see him as one among a number of important religious leaders. Some feminists, such as Rosemary Radford Ruether, ask, "Can a male savior save women?"[1] They reject using Jesus' maleness as the basis for perpetuating male-dominated theologies and structures, but experience grace in his consistent compassion for the poor and marginalized, who frequently were women. Others object to seeing Jesus as a champion of our existing culture. They stress his place at the forefront of change, calling us out of self-preoccupation toward the forgotten or emerging parts of society.[2]

Titles given to Jesus raise further questions. Contemporary critics question using monarchical or hierarchical titles such as *king* or *lord*, claiming they foster imperial understandings of religion. They prefer such terms as *brother* and *friend* to stress the community of equals that Jesus fostered.[3]

These questions are challenging and important. They are in our minds as we present aspects of Jesus that, in the midst of these questions, have continuing relevance for us today.

PREFACE TO
THE DOORWAYS SERIES

Two of us were rambling along a trail on a sparkling spring day. One was discouraged, did not know where her life was going. The other felt content and grateful for time to see what was happening in the woods.

Suddenly we stopped. Across our path lay a branch, broken off and seemingly dead. But there right on that branch burst forth a blossom that beamed at us in greeting.

We looked at each other and smiled. In that flower, God had broken in on us with a message: life can burst forth unexpectedly and bless us with its presence.

This brief story came to mind as we were thinking about the purpose of the four books in the *Doorways* Series. They are for people with hope, energy, and commitment who want reinforcement. They also are for dispirited people who question the direction of their own lives and of society.

The books invite you to taste nourishing spiritual food discovered by people in one particular faith path—the Christian tradition. From the core of this tradition radiates an astounding truth: there is at the heart of the universe a cherishing presence that holds all creation in a loving embrace. To be nurtured by this love is to be infused by fresh life.

In a fast-moving, multifaceted society, people look for anchors to hold them steady. Mobility makes us long for a sense of belonging. Pressing personal and societal needs make us wonder where we fit and how we can contribute.

The *Doorways* Series was written in response to these yearnings. It helps us listen to our own truth and to sink our roots in a

solid tradition. It takes us on a journey of discovery. Its purpose is
to help us grow in spiritual awareness, learn to build community
where we are, and be more fully God's person at home, at work,
and in the other places where we spend our time.

Underneath our yearnings are profound questions. Each book
in the *Doorways* Series focuses on one question most of us ask at
one time or another:

✤ Who is God?

✤ Who is Jesus?

✤ How can I nourish my spirit?

✤ What should I do with my life?

To aid you in addressing these questions, this series offers
twenty-four dynamic stories, images, and concepts found in the
Christian tradition. When you allow your body, mind, and spirit
to engage with these treasures, you will be enlarged, enhanced,
empowered.

Included in each book are activities for you, the reader, as
well as for a group. Thus, each book can be used as a course. Designed originally by a community of Catholic and Protestant
laypeople, the courses include wisdom and practices from each
tradition that we have found powerful in our own lives. The
courses build on each other, but each can be used on its own.

In their time with Jesus, the disciples had a training experience—living, learning, doing. They moved from being neophytes
to well-trained healers and teachers. These courses are designed to
replicate this experience of growth for us twentieth-century
people, to equip us to live the committed life. Each of the *Doorways* courses presents a different challenge.

Encountering God in the Old Testament provides a way to explore the understandings of God realized by people in the Old Testament. This introductory course is suited to people with no prior experience of faith as well as to longtime churchgoers who are taking another look at the meaning of faith.

Meeting Jesus in the New Testament offers opportunities to learn about the Jesus of history and to make faith decisions today in response to the living presence of the Spirit. It is for those who want to be more than observers of the ministry of Jesus, who want to explore being companions in that work.

Journeying with the Spirit is for those who are committed to the way of Jesus and who would like to strengthen that commitment through experiencing classic resources for growth such as prayer, meditation, healing, and reconciliation.

Discovering Your Gifts, Vision, and Call is for people concerned with the pain and disharmony in the world and who want to help implement God's vision for the world. It offers a discernment process for discovering one's gifts and calling as well as ideas for forming communities to give communal expression to it.

These four courses are progressive in that they build on a deepening relationship with God and provide opportunities to:

✦ *explore* experiences of God;

✦ *decide* about one's relationship to God;

✦ *deepen* those decisions;

✦ *discern* life direction and purpose.

We offer these books to each of you as you seek to find your particular way of making the world a better place. If current environmental degradation teaches anything, it is that every person on Earth must become involved in preserving this precious creation. To build the kind of global resolve necessary will require commitment and stamina, which come from being firmly rooted in sources of spiritual power.

HOW TO USE THIS BOOK
AS A COURSE

This book is designed not only to be read but to be used as a course for individuals and groups. As an individual, you can gain much from "doing" this book in your own way and in your own timing. Adapt the Group Design exercises to yourself and try them out. Do the Individual Work. Perhaps you can find another person with whom to share the course or to discuss some of its aspects. If you are motivated to work alone with the content, honor that instinct and have confidence that your efforts will bear fruit.

Groups that can benefit from the material are existing Bible-study, life-sharing, or task groups who want to grow together, or groups especially convened for the particular training offered through these courses.

✤ How the Material Is Organized ✤

Each book includes an introduction, six sessions, and ideas for further reflection and next steps. Each of the six sessions includes:

✤ Session Text: basic content material on the topic;

✤ Group Design: practical ways for a group to work with the content in the session text;

✤ Individual Work: suggestions on how to apply the content to our own lives as individuals.

✤ Using the Material in Groups ✤

In order to get the most from the course, it is important to do three things:

1. Read and Digest the Text. Before coming to the first meeting, read the introduction, How to Use This Book as a Course, and the Session 1 text in preparation. To prepare for the second session, read the text for Session 2, and so on through the six sessions of the book. It is best to devote most of your time between meetings to the Individual Work related to the preceding session before reading the new session. Leave the new session for the day or so before you meet.

2. Participate in the Group Design. When people relax and participate in the group activities, much growth occurs. No design is perfect, and no design works equally well for all groups. Don't be bound by these design ideas, but do take time to understand their underlying purpose. If you can accomplish the same goals in other ways, great. You may want to modify the timing on the designs. We estimate that our timing works easily for groups of about twelve people. Smaller groups will have more time; larger groups may have to shorten or omit certain activities.

Each Group Design has several parts that we will look at in detail.

Gathering Time: The purpose of this is to assemble the group and ready yourselves for the session. Since we have built in ways to share personal information throughout the design, this does not have to be accomplished fully in the gathering time. Ten minutes is usually sufficient. Divide the time equally among all of you and really listen to each person. Resist the temptation to allow more time for this section or to be undisciplined in its use.

Sharing Groups: These are groups of four that you form at the first session. The purpose of these is to share in a small setting what you did with the suggestions for Individual Work and to support one another as you take the course. These same groups meet at least once during each session. We find there are many benefits when the same group meets consistently. To get to know others in the larger group, there will be activities to do with them as well.

Discussion of the Session Text: We have included discussion of the text only occasionally because we felt it useful to give more time to other activities. However, if your group would like to discuss it each time, feel free to do so. Here's a sample discussion question: What learning from the text was most important for you?

Lab Exercise: The purpose of the lab exercise is to enable the group to experience one aspect of the topic and reflect on this experience. The activities in this section vary a great deal. Some are lighthearted, while others are more serious. Participants have found them to be valuable.

Closing: This time is meant to give people an opportunity to reflect on the session and to have closure. Sometimes we offer a suggestion about how to do this; at other times we leave it to you. Some groups like to vary their closing exercises; others like the consistency of the same ending each time, such as a favorite song or a circle of prayer.

Materials: We suggest that you bring a Bible and a notebook for each session. When additional materials are needed, this is indicated in the design.

Breaks: According to your group's needs, schedule a five- to ten-minute break in the middle of each session. Our estimated timing does not include breaks, so adjust your timing accordingly. Tell people at the beginning of the session when the break will be.

3. Do the Individual Work. This work is designed to be done at home between sessions and is an important part of the course. It is a bridge between sessions and provides ways for you to integrate the material. Our participants find this one of the most worthwhile parts of the experience and urge us to underscore its importance.

The individual work usually involves fifteen to thirty minutes of quiet time per day for reading, reflection, and writing your thoughts in a journal, usually a loose-leaf notebook. At the end of each week it is useful to write a one-paragraph summary of what you did, your particular learnings and difficulties, and any questions. This summary can be shared with the group.

We suggest that you devote the quiet times during the first part of your week to the Individual Work and that you use the last few days before your group session to read the new chapter in preparation for the next session.

For the six weeks of the course, budget the time you need to do the Individual Work. It is integral to the course.

✣ What About Leadership? ✣

Don't rely on just one person to make your group thrive. Leadership is needed for two functions: *facilitation* and *organization*. Consider finding two people for each function. Choose these people on the basis of gifts and motivation. Who would really like to do what?

Facilitation: This can be done by the same person or pair each time or rotated so everyone in the group takes a turn. As the group facilitator you will:

✣ read the session text, Group Design, and Individual Work in advance;

✤ gather the necessary materials for the next session;

✤ convene the group at the start of the session;

✤ lead it through the Group Design, keeping to the time you agree on;

✤ close the meeting with a reminder of the time and place of the next session.

There are additional ways you as a facilitator can help the group. You might:

✤ do some background reading.

✤ add your creativity to the Group Design, tailoring it to the needs of the group.

✤ pray for the people in the group.

✤ give examples from your own life to begin sharing times. The way you do this modeling is important. If your example is long, other people's examples will be long. If you share from the heart, others are likely to do the same. By your example you give others freedom to be open. Our participants tell us that when they hear leaders share authentic pains and joys, they feel encouraged to face similar feelings in their own situations.

✤ be attentive to nonverbal communication in the group. As a leader, you can foster an atmosphere of caring, genuineness, and openness through a smile, a word of encouragement, a touch on the arm.

Organization: This, too, can be done by the same person or pair each time, or rotated. To help in this way you can:

✤ publicize the course by placing notices in newsletters, making personal phone calls to invite people to attend, and distributing flyers;

✤ be attentive during the session to people's reactions and lend encouragement to those who need it;

✤ call absent people between times to fill them in on what happened;

✤ see that refreshments are provided, if the group wishes them;

✤ pray for the individuals in the group.

We call the organization people *shepherds* since they look after and care for each person individually, leaving the facilitators free to care about group process and content. After facilitating courses with the assistance of shepherds, we would never be without them. They make a major difference in the quality and depth of a course. Shepherding is a wonderful gift that some people have and enjoy using.

✤ How to Gather a Group ✤

Suppose you would like to gather a group to take a *Doorways* course together. Find another person who will work with you and who has enthusiasm about doing the course. Consider whether to seek church sponsorship. To find people who would like to take the course and to prepare them to participate fully, you can do these things:

1. *Spread the word as widely as possible*.

Start with family, friends, neighbors, members of groups active in the church and community, and newcomers. Try to contact these people personally. Tell them the purposes of the course: to provide spiritual nourishment, to build a caring and supportive group, and to discover which part of God's work we are called to foster. (To become clearer about the purpose for the course, read the introductory material in the beginning of the course.)

People respond to an invitation to join the course for a variety of reasons: some are looking for a sense of belonging; others want purpose or direction in their lives; others are hungry for spiritual nourishment. Find out what people are looking for and then describe how the course addresses that need.

2. *Be sure to go over procedural matters such as the dates, time, and place for the course.*

If possible, try to hold the course in a comfortable, home-like atmosphere.

Explain that the course depends on the commitment of all the members to come regularly, to be on time, to do the Individual Work, and to let someone know if they will be absent so they can be brought up-to-date before the next session.

3. *Let people know that the method used will be experiential learning.*

This style depends on the participation of each person and not on the expertise of a leader. Participants learn by doing. You each proceed at your own pace and in your own way. Some people will have important insights during the group meetings; others may have them at home; others may see results from the course only after it has ended.

This style of learning contrasts with traditional ways of teaching in which someone in authority (a theologian, pastor, or teacher) offers content to a learner, whose main job is to assimilate and apply it. Some people may expect a traditional approach and ask questions such as "Who's teaching the course? Who's the leader?" Sometimes we offer this explanation: The traditional approach is useful for imparting doctrine (the wisdom and teachings of the church throughout history). Experiential learning enables us to examine some of those doctrines and make them a living part of our lives. The facilitators of the course are learners with all the others who take it.

    4. *Pray together for the group.*

    That can make the difference between gratitude and frustration in gathering a group. When you pray, you may be given inspiration about new people to contact or new ways to do it.

    5. *Determine the size and makeup of the group.*

    The course works well with groups numbering from ten to twenty, people of all ages, clergy and laity, men and women.

SESSION 1

Immanuel/God with Us

Jesus is first introduced to us by the early Christians as a helpless baby, born to a poor couple in an obscure village in an occupied country.

In the nativity narratives, the mixed responses to the baby are presented in starkly contrasting images and pictures. Mary and Joseph welcome, hold, love, and provide for the child. The presence of the animals symbolizes the natural world as an important part of God's revelation. Leaving their ordinary concerns, and guided by a vision of angels, the shepherds come to adore the infant. Three wise men, representing the three races of humankind—European, Asiatic, and African—come bearing symbolic gifts: gold as a tribute to Christ the royal person, frankincense in homage to the divinity Christ represents, and myrrh, foretelling Jesus' suffering and death.

In contrast to this care, adoration, and giving is the jealousy and brutality of Herod. As a ruler, he can stand no other claims to leadership and therefore vents his rage in one of the cruelest acts in history, the slaughter of Israel's firstborn sons. This unspeakable crime forces the family of Jesus into a refugee existence in Egypt and tightens the Roman oppression of the people of Israel.

The nativity story is retold around the world each year. Its theological implications have been explained in various ways. The central message is that God is personal and intimately *with us*—not a distant God who winds up the world and then lets it run on its own, but a God who wants to be as close to us as a newborn infant is to its parents.

To begin our exploration of Jesus, we relate to him first as tiny, vulnerable child. To understand the significance of Jesus' coming to us as a baby, we first look at what people were expecting. Biblical scholar John Bright describes the Hebrews' longing for the establishment of God's realm. Their hope was expressed in different ways. The Zealots, the nationalist party within Judaism, hoped for the "political restoration of independence from Rome through military action led by the Messiah." The Pharisees, members of a religious group that believed in strict observance of the written and oral law, held to the ideal of a Holy Commonwealth that would come through God's action combined with the people's careful adherence to the law. The apocalypticists yearned for the catastrophic intervention of God, when the heavens would open to reveal a divine one descending on clouds to earth (Dan. 7:13).[1]

Political independence, military victory, and religious purity concerned various groups of Hebrew people. They yearned for a strong military leader, a righteous king, or a supernatural figure to intervene and bring greatness to their nation.

Yet the long-awaited one appears first as a baby, shattering lofty expectations and requiring a response that comes not from prestige or power but from an open heart.

This response of the heart to Jesus as a baby comes alive each year at the Christmas Eve family service in our church. Most of the time, our congregation would be characterized by its intellectual sophistication and its concern for social and political action. But during this service we express quite another side of ourselves. The mother, father, and newest baby in the congregation are asked to form a living crèche in our chancel. At a certain point in the service, as Christmas carols are sung, all are invited into the chancel to be with "the holy family." The new baby evokes marvelous responses: smiles, cooing, sometimes tears, and a general nonverbal communication that for a few moments makes us feel at one with the family, one another, and with God in a delightful circle of love.

Recent brain research has elucidated differences between the logical, analytical left side of the brain and the right hemisphere, which is at home with fantasy, dreams, and intuitions. Before our own "holy family," it is as if for one moment the world stands still and we as a congregation are capable of whole-brain knowing, a true wedding of heart and mind. We receive in our hearts that evening what all year long we struggle to understand in our minds: that at the center of the universe is a love so personal that it has the capacity to call forth a similar love from each person who will engage with it.

It is as if God, like a Zen master, has struck the Earth with a wholly unexpected illumination: *God comes to us in the form of a baby!* Along with being transcendent, God is approachable, vulnerable, and needs and wants our response of love—first heart to heart, and gradually mind to mind.

We may have other ideas about Jesus' meaning for us. In the first Group Design, there is time to share our expectations of Jesus for this period of our lives. What do we hope for? Some people believe that contact with Jesus will help them make sense of the universe so that they will have a clearer purpose for their life. Others yearn for a deeper sense of belonging to the family of God and hope that relating in a personal way to Jesus can help them find that. Still others see Jesus as a liberator of the oppressed and look for empowerment in the work of social justice. Do we all come to Jesus wanting or looking for something, when in reality God is trying to show us through the baby the importance of simply being with Jesus, allowing the wonder of the baby to penetrate our being? Perhaps, like his parents, we are invited to hold the baby and the reality he represents. Maybe that will call forth the giving of ourselves and our gifts as it did for the wise men.

But do we know how to do that—to allow ourselves simply to be with Jesus? Perhaps in our producer–consumer society many have lost that capacity. Tilden Edwards, Episcopal priest and writer, is dedicated to helping us recover the ability simply to be. He points out that "increasingly the cultural norm [is] moving between a kind of driven work time and a very narrow escapist rest time which often isn't very restful."[2]

To counter this, Edwards suggests that we find times when we cultivate an appreciation of life as a gift rather than as "a curse or something that has to be made over all the time."[3] Such a time can be termed Sabbath time. We allow ourselves to slow down, to have more space and less "stuff," e.g., words, activity. We can create such a time for a few moments every day or several times a day as well as setting aside longer times for this purpose.

Many of the saints found and used Sabbath time well. They were given to much listening, pondering, absorbing, and often to few words. Two of the words St. Ignatius used most frequently in prayer were *"Mira! Mira!"* or "Look! Look!" That was the way he contemplated the mystery of Christ.[4] The prayer of Francis for nights on end was simply: "Who are you, O God? And who am I?"[5]

A friend once shared the secret of his appreciation of great paintings. He would spend his first moments in a gallery taking in the sweep of the exhibit. Then, choosing a favorite painting, he spent an hour simply absorbing the great work, letting it speak to him. Many people appreciate nature in the same way. Rather than analyzing a flower, they simply look at it and allow its beauty to nourish their spirits. This is how we can approach Jesus. Look, absorb, appreciate. Allow the infant Jesus to nourish your spirit. Let the experience of his coming as baby take on a deeper reality for you.

When we allow ourselves quiet time and disengagement from the busyness of our world, we may realize that the characters in the nativity story not only belong in the scene two thousand years ago. They reside in us as well. The same mixed reaction to the divine gift exists inside as well as outside ourselves. Part of us is willing to allow the infant to call forth our heart response, and part of us is threatened by it. We may offer our intellect, love, and suffering as gifts to Jesus, but then keep a running account of what we are getting out of it. If the infant Jesus resides in a shabby place or at a great distance from where we are, we may prefer to stay home and read the paper.

Nevertheless, the welcome mat is out. God invites us to receive a gift: divine love in human form, and to begin with, in that most lovable of forms—as a baby.

GROUP DESIGN

Purpose: To become acquainted with one another, share our expectations of Jesus for this period of our lives, and experience the wonder of God's coming to us as a human infant.

Materials: Baby photos (preferably large), Christmas carols (see D, Closing).

A. Gathering Time, Large Group (*twenty minutes*)

To get acquainted and begin to think about the birth of Jesus, share your name and remembrance of a birthday, either yours or that of someone else. Use about a minute per person.

For example, "My name is Carlos Diaz. I remember a recent birthday when my friend, who knew that I loved a certain author, arranged for a private showing of a movie about that person at

the public library. Then we had a good time watching it together."

B. Sharing Groups, Groups of Four (*thirty minutes*)

Move into groups of four so that you are with people you do
not know well. Share names and phone numbers. Jot them in a
notebook for ready reference. Then briefly speak about what you
hope will happen personally as a result of your contact with Jesus
through this course. This is not an easy topic, so take a few minutes
of silence to think about it, perhaps writing down a few thoughts in
your notebook. Then briefly share these hopes. You may want to
write down key hopes next to people's names so you can hold these
in your thoughts or prayer. For example, "Jim hopes to grow beyond his childhood image of Jesus as meek and mild."

Note on sharing: Make it personal and relevant to the question. If you do not have a response to a particular question or prefer not to share one, feel free to "pass." Remind one another of
these suggestions as needed.

C. Experiencing Jesus as a Baby, Large Group
  Meditation (*sixty minutes*)

1. *Focal point:* In order to help people get in the mood for
meditating on Jesus as a baby, display in the center of your circle
some baby pictures of family or friends. Larger pictures are easier
to see. Enjoy looking at them for a few minutes. The idea is to create an atmosphere of openness toward the infant. Then settle into
a comfortable position for meditation, with pen and paper in
hand. The leader will read the first paragraph of the meditation,
and then say, "Respond." Allow yourself to respond as deeply as
possible to what was read. Then, if you wish, jot down what comes

to your mind or heart. In this type of meditation, some people have much to write; for others, a word or two is sufficient.

2. *Meditation read by one person in a slow and relaxed fashion:* "In order to move into our meditation, take a few minutes to relax and settle into a comfortable position. (*Pause.*) Take a few slow deep breaths. (*Pause.*) Allow silence to deepen among us. (*Pause.*) We may be more aware of the noises around us. Let the noises be, even as we allow a silent, centered atmosphere to en- velop us. (*Pause.*)

"The procedure for our meditation is this. I'll read a short paragraph, and then say 'Respond.' At that time let your mind and heart respond as freely as possible. Then, if you wish, write your response in your notebook. It may be anything from 'Yes, I want to be open' to 'I'm having trouble concentrating.' Even though you may be tired and have other things on your mind, bring yourself before God as you are. Be ready to hear something within yourself that comes from a deeper level. Now I'll begin."

✦ Infancy Meditation ✦

"I have come, am born, of an unknown girl in an obscure town. I come at an inconvenient time. While they are journeying far from home, I arrive. My mother wraps me in something warm and lays me in a manger. She and Joseph surround me with their love, give themselves to caring for me. Can I come to you like that: unexpectedly? inconveniently? Respond. (*Reader pause for several minutes, allowing time for others to jot down thoughts.*)

"My angel appears to men on a hillside, . . . says, 'Don't worry, I have great news. . . . He has come.' Those rough, simple, tired men leave their valuable flocks. They trust, believe, hurry to my side. I send my messengers to you also. Do you recognize them? Respond. (*Reader pause as above.*)

"Not everyone is happy that I have come. Although I am a helpless, tiny babe, a king is threatened by my birth. He plots against me. Human nature is many-sided. Does a part of you feel threatened, too? Does it seek ways to avoid me? Respond. (*Reader pause*.)

"Three wise seekers, people of science, of wealth, come looking for me. They have left safe and predictable lives, positions that are highly regarded. They have left all this to search for me over rough, lonely roads. You, too, have comfortable positions, certain kinds of security. Are you willing to seek me over difficult paths? Respond. (*Reader pause*.)

"This is the end of the meditation. Slowly return your attention to this room."

3. *Sharing:*

    a. In the group of four you were in before, go around the circle and share briefly what happened in this meditation as you thought about Jesus as baby. Let each person have a turn; refrain from commenting. Focus on what did or did not happen during this meditation, not on opinions or questions out of the past. If you prefer not to share, say "Pass."

    b. Large group: You may want to finish in the large group with any insights or experiences that seemed particularly helpful in the small group. This can also be a time for those who had trouble getting into the meditation to ask for some suggestions.

D. Closing, Large Group (*ten minutes*)

Choose one or two of the following suggestions as appropriate for your group:

1. Evaluate this session. (In a few words, what was helpful? What was not helpful?)

2. Sing (Christmas carols such as "What Child Is This?" or "O Little Town of Bethlehem").

3. Pray.

4. Discuss details of next session if necessary (time, place, leadership responsibility).

INDIVIDUAL WORK

If you are working alone with the course material, use the Infancy Meditation from section C, item 2 in the Group Design once or twice before moving on to the following exercise.

Purpose: To establish a time to be alone with God, to meditate on the beginning of Jesus' life and work, and to use some of the processes he went through to reflect on where we are and what we want to be about in our own lives.

Note: This individual work forms a bridge between our contemplation of Jesus' infancy and his public life.

1. *Meditate:* This week we invite you to meditate on the initial steps of Jesus' public life and work as described in Matt. 3:13–17; Luke 3:21–23, Luke 4, and Luke 5:1–11. First read these passages. Spend some time gaining a deeper sense of what happened in these strange and surprising events. Be there with Jesus, in his shoes (sandals!). Try to share his thoughts and feelings.

2. *Read:* "The Beginning of Jesus' Public Ministry," beginning on page 27.

3. *Write:* Ponder and then write your answers to the questions on these topics taken from "The Beginning of Jesus' Public Ministry." You may wish to concentrate on one or two topics that seem most relevant to you.

a. Baptism: For Jesus, it was a time of showing publicly that he was dedicated to embodying God's love and justice. How would you describe yourself at this point in your life? To what are you dedicated? Would it be important to say something aloud about this to someone?

b. Temptation: What throws you off course from the way you feel that God and your own deep energy call you to go?

c. Articulation: Can you articulate the purpose of your life and work? Is there a passage of scripture that helps you describe it?

d. Reactions: How do you deal with the reactions of others as you try to discern and be true to God's direction?

e. The Call for Company: What kind of companionship do you want or need as you seek to deepen your journey with God?

As we can see, for Jesus launching the new way had different elements, each of which was important. So the launching or relaunching of God's way in us may require different steps. No two people are in precisely the same spot. As you ponder the steps mentioned above, be conscious of which seem most important at this time in your life.

4. *Summarize:* At the end of the week, summarize in writing what you did with this assignment. Be brief, honest, and to the point. This will help you consolidate your feelings and learning and prepare you for the next session. When you have done this, read the text for Session 2.

✤ The Beginning of Jesus' Public Ministry ✤

Name: Jesus
Age: Thirty
Home Address: Nazareth
Occupation: Carpenter
Education: Scripture study in home and synagogue; on-the-job training in carpentry with father.

Not a very impressive résumé, but this is all we know of the person who was about to begin a second career that changed the world forever. Before we contemplate the content and the outcome of that career, it is important to look at the circumstances of Jesus' life and try to see their meaning not only for Jesus but for us. He left the security of a known family, a recognized address, and an easy-to-understand occupation to be with strangers whose only affinity was that they said yes to his call. Led by the Spirit, he ventured out, with no sure place to lay his head, and began a life and work whose depth and meaning have never been exhausted in two thousand years of analysis. The thirtieth year of his life, as he moved from a private to a public existence, was a turning point.

What was the nature of this turning point? How did he get started? Did he know what to do readily, or did he have to struggle to figure it out? The Gospel writers supply us with some details, the meaning and implications of which are well worth pondering.

Baptism: Jesus' first public act was to be baptized by John. Why? Jesus had a sense of destiny, a special background of blessing by parents and insightful religious people, and an awareness of being called to a life of love and service. Yet he submitted to the ministry of a lesser person, one who saw himself as the usher of a new way but who had a limited understanding of its meaning. Moreover, John was using baptism to signify that one had turned away from sin and toward a new relationship with God. Did Jesus need that? Even John was puzzled by Jesus' request, but Jesus asked him to "give in for now."

While we do not know why Jesus took this step, we can make certain observations. It did show that Jesus affirmed John's insistence that recognizing and turning away from whatever keeps us from God is a condition for entering a fuller, more fruitful life of love and justice. It did, in fact, usher in a new life for Jesus. Moreover, it was a conscious, witnessed declaration of his intent, a time when he came into a new identity and expressed it publicly. As Jesus emerged from the river, two important ratifications of this step occurred. The Bible reports that a voice from heaven assured him he was beloved by God, and a dove appeared, which he took as a sign of God's blessing of that moment.

Temptations: One would think that with that auspicious start, Jesus would have plunged into his public career. But the opposite is true. He went off by himself to the desert to think through everything. What happened there? The Bible says, "he was tempted by the devil" (Luke 4:2, NAB). Right on the heels of a sublime feeling of blessing at baptism, he is tempted to misuse his power, love, and insight. Which of the many messianic expectations of his people would he emphasize and try to fulfill? Political power, material security, or dramatic indications of God's presence—all of these were options to consider, but he rejected them to focus on the simple, uncompromising love of God and its availability to all without exception.

Articulation of the Mission: What then, in the deprivation of the wilderness, was the path Jesus decided to take? Both there and later in the synagogue, he went to Scripture for insight and direction. He countered each temptation with a powerful scriptural expression of the direction he felt led to take by the Spirit. Then, in the synagogue, he publicly expressed that mission and ministry. To do it, he used the words of Isa. 61:1–2, one of the songs of the Suffering Servant.

The Reaction of the People: One might think that with all the thought and prayer that went into Jesus' statement of purpose, preceded by the blessing received at his baptism, the reaction of the people would be one of unanimous approval. But again we are surprised. The reactions are extremely mixed: They run the gamut from adulation to rejection, from welcome to resistance, from wonder to fright. If Jesus needed or planned to take his cues from people's reactions, he would have been thrown into total confusion. But this was not the case. He was able, as the Bible puts it, "to walk through the crowd and go on his way."

The Call of the Disciples: The strength that came from wrestling with all the alternatives, from spending long periods in prayer and discernment, and finally from declaring who he was and what he was about made it possible for Jesus to stand alone. He could teach with authority and effectiveness, heal people's spiritual and physical problems, and bring good news to the many he touched. He could go it alone. But he chose not to do that. Very quickly he selected companions and proceeded to share his ministry with them through an intensive living/learning experience. These persons, whom he later called friends, apparently had no special qualities that fitted them for this work. Their only qualification seemed to be that they responded to his call, his invitation, to "follow me." He accepted that response without question and gave himself to forming them into bearers of good news.

SESSION 2

Healer/Liberator

Jesus made his first public appearance in Nazareth, his home-town, after his solitary time in the desert. In the synagogue where he regularly worshiped, he did something that so angered some of the townsfolk that they dragged him out of the city and threatened to throw him over a cliff.

What caused such a violent reaction? Jesus had begun by reading aloud from one of the most sacred Hebrew Scriptures, the Song of the Servant as expressed in Isaiah:

> The Spirit of the Lord is upon me . . .
> to preach good news to the poor. . . .
> to proclaim release to the captives
> and recovering of sight to the blind,
> to set at liberty those who are oppressed,
> to proclaim the acceptable year of the Lord.
> (*Luke 4:18–19*, RSV)

Jesus used this passage to describe his own mission. He caught the attention of his listeners by concluding: "Today this Scripture passage is fulfilled in your hearing" (Luke 4:21, NAB).

At this point, Luke reports a favorable response from the assembly: "And he won the approval of all, and they were astonished by the gracious words that came from his lips" (Luke 4:22, NAB).

But Jesus' next words aroused a ferocious reaction. His mission was to include those beyond the accepted boundaries, the foreign widow and leper. These were people his listeners despised! Believing themselves special in God's sight, they felt foreigners to be excluded from God's love. And here was Jesus saying they were included.

Jesus' inclusiveness toward those on the outside upset people then and does today. Why should the poor receive good news? They deserve their poverty! Why should captives be released? Criminals and challengers of the prevailing political system are best kept under lock and key. And whoever heard of the blind receiving sight? Isn't most blindness permanent? Why should the oppressed be set free? Isn't their passivity and laziness responsible for their condition?

A disturbing and provocative way to begin a public ministry! No wonder people wanted to get rid of him. Not only did Jesus make startling statements, his actions amazed people.

Gathering companions in carrying out his mission, Jesus began his ministry by healing people from disease and freeing them from what held them captive. Luke records:

> Now when the sun was setting, all those who had any
> that were sick with various diseases brought them to
> him; and he laid his hands on every one of them and
> healed them. (Luke 4:40, RSV)

The deaf heard, the blind saw, the paralyzed walked, the possessed were freed. People were healed emotionally or physically and liberated from disease, fear, sin, oppression. Reactions varied: joy, relief, surprise, confusion.

This session focuses on Jesus' ministry of healing and liberation and asks how it is embodied today. How do we participate in it?

In dozens of ways. When a father bandages the knee of his injured toddler, when a nurse holds a patient's hand, when a researcher isolates a newly discovered virus, when a community organizer mobilizes tenants to fight unfair rental rates, when a student learns about a different culture, when a negotiator forges an agreement for arms reduction—these are times when God's healing and liberation can occur in our complicated world. Listen to the stories of people we know who are agents of healing and liberation today.

As a manager of policy and programs in the Agency for International Development, Jerry Kamens engages in activities that bring freedom from conflict and poverty: conflict resolution between Arabs and Israelis; creation of joint agricultural programs that teach disparate groups to work together; water purification projects that remove the threat of high infant mortality. He seeks to reconcile opposing needs. "I look for ways to protect the environment for our grandchildren but also to help farmers increase production so they have enough to live on today."

Joan Cooper, the mother of a son imprisoned for drug use, has joined with a Baptist minister in taking action against drug addiction and dealing in her neighborhood. Each night she had listened to rising violence, even gunshots. Mobilizing neighbors and public officials, she launched a nightly "Citizens' Patrol." Risking retaliation by dealers and addicts, patrol members photographed actions, recorded license numbers, and reported information to the police. For a year and a half this core of people has held firm, joined sporadically by other community leaders. Prevention and treatment programs have increased. Although the problem is far from solved, Joan's determination has inspired many. Asked where she gets her courage, she replied, "I am committed to Christ. He is in me, and I am in him."

For years Judy Funderburk, a creative movement specialist, struggled with bulimia, an eating disorder. Psychological and medical interventions failed to heal her disturbing symptoms. Finally, recognizing how drawn she was to movement, she joined a dance workshop that invited participants to depict deep feelings through movement and drawing. So powerful were her learnings that Judy continued on this path, finally earning a master's degree in expressive arts therapy. This approach to healing, she says, helps us access "our body's stories—the images and memories held in our cells. Movement, visualization, journaling, and drawing are some of the processes that help us confront what blocks our full experience of life." She has learned that physical movement, repeated and pushed to the edge of former patterns, often releases repressed images, feelings, thoughts, and spiritual longings. Giving form to this deep physical release through the expressive arts makes it possible to work with one's inner life, bringing healing and wholeness. "As one draws, sounds, enacts, or dances out that which has been released," she writes, "it can begin to be named, confronted, encompassed, or cast out."[1]

People like these are inspiring and challenging. Yet sometimes their courage and commitment are so strong that we feel discouraged by our seeming weakness. How can we participate in the healing and liberation Jesus brought about? Close attention to one of the healing stories of Jesus provides some answers. It begins with failure. The father of a boy stricken with epilepsy asked Jesus' disciples to cure him. When they could not do it, everyone crowded around, arguing heatedly. Jesus approached and asked what was happening. The boy's father told him of the disciples' inability to heal his son. Brought before Jesus, the boy had another frightening convulsion. "If you can do anything," the father begged, "have pity on us and help us." Jesus replied, "If you can! All things are possible to him who believes." The father cried out, "I believe. Help my unbelief" (Mark 9:14–24, RSV).

It is not hard to see ourselves in this story. Like the father, we may have asked someone for help only to be disappointed. Or, like the disciples, we may have offered help or healing to another, but with no apparent results. Or like the boy, nearly all of us at one time or another have felt severely incapacitated—unable to relate to others, to ourselves, or to God. What is powerful about this story is that the father, despite previous disappointment, tried again. He acted not on his doubt but on his hope and belief, and thus brought the boy directly to Jesus. It is much like the well-known advice given to those who would like to believe in God but do not know how to begin: give as much of yourself as you can to as much of God as you know. This is what the father did.

Our sessions provide opportunity to experience this story and to open ourselves to the healing or liberating we need. Today it is easier to imagine that healing can occur than it was even twenty years ago. Science and medicine are moving toward a holistic concept of healing. Cancer researchers experiment with guided imagery as an aid to healing patients. In *An Anatomy of an Illness*, Norman Cousins describes how he used humor in a self-healing process that cured him of a degenerative disease.[2] Current brain research underlines the importance of the body/mind connection. To hope for healing and to visualize it happening is recommended by people in many fields. Ministries for physical and spiritual healing are increasingly available in churches. An experiment to verify the effects of prayer for healing at San Francisco General Hospital was reported in *Newsweek:*

> A researcher asked outsiders to pray for a group of cardiac patients. Even though the patients weren't told that prayers were being said for them, the study found that they recovered faster than those in an otherwise identical control group.[3]

There is an element of mystery in healing that no amount of human understanding can fathom. Moreover, there are plenty of blocks to belief in the healing power of Jesus' love. Stories of ill people prayed for who continue to suffer, instances of brutality and cruelty, and our own hurts and disappointments prevent us from reaching out for healing, freedom, and newness. We are tempted to act on our skepticism and unbelief.

Yet if Jesus is to be believed, God does not passively wait for us, but stirs our yearnings for liberation and healing, reaches toward us, offering fullness of life. God invites us to come, see, and experience.

What is required is openness—both to our blind spots and to the healing and inner freedom that closer contact with God can bring.

These do not always happen in the way we expect or through the means we might choose. Yet aligning ourselves with God's power is one of the most important things we do for ourselves, our loved ones, and for the world.

Attending to our own needs for healing and liberation—whether physical, emotional, or spiritual—brings us back full circle to where we began this chapter. Jesus saw the Reign of God as a new order for persons and for society. Studies of the student reformers of the 1960s show that as their plans for world reform were not realized, many suffered burnout. Some now state that they had nothing within to sustain them. They now realize that the road to social transformation must include personal transformation. There seems to be an ageless wisdom in Jesus' starting his plan for universal re-formation with the healing and liberation of individuals.

GROUP DESIGN

Purpose: To share what we did with the Individual Work for Session 1, to discuss the relevance of Jesus' liberation and healing, and to open ourselves to the Spirit's healing within.

Materials: Bibles, candle, oil, cross, small tables, record of meditative music.

A. Gathering Time, Large Group (*ten minutes*)

Begin in a way that involves everyone, including any newcomers. This might be a prayer or a brief sharing of an important moment in your week.

B. Sharing Groups, Groups of Four
(twenty minutes)

This is the time to describe briefly what you did with the suggestions for Individual Work at the end of Session 1 and how they affected you: your insights, feelings, difficulties. Give each person a chance to speak without interruption, comment, or discussion before opening up for free conversation. Remember, you are free to pass if you prefer.

C. Discussion of the Session Text, Large Group
(thirty-five minutes)

Read Luke 4:18–19 and consider these questions for discussion:

✤ Where do you see God's liberating action at work today?

✤ How are you personally participating or failing to participate in liberation?

✤ What causes you to seek healing from God?

✤ What factors block your belief in God's healing power today?

D. Experience of Healing and Liberation, Large Group (forty-five minutes)

Preparation: Place a lighted candle in the center of the circle as a focus. Perhaps you could add an object or two that symbolizes God's healing (for example, a small container of oil, a cross, a Bible). If you wish, play some meditative music for a few minutes to help you relax. Sit in a comfortable position with notebook and pen at hand. A member reads Mark 9:14–29 slowly, then reads the following meditation.

✤ Meditation ✤

"Now I will help bring the story to life with a few questions. After each, I will say 'Respond' and then pause. This is the time for meditation and, if we wish, for recording some of our thoughts and feelings in our journals. These thoughts will not be shared; they are for ourselves alone.

"First, imagine you are in the crowd arguing with the scribes. You see Jesus coming, and you run excitedly toward him. You hear the father's complaint and see his son. You hear Jesus' strong assurance that, of course, he can help the boy. Then you hear Jesus command the deaf and dumb spirit to come out of the boy and never go into him again. You see the boy collapse. Then you witness Jesus lifting him up. The boy stands on his own two feet and finally walks off. How do you feel? Respond. (*Pause.*)

"Now imagine you are the boy . . . incapacitated in some way. Think of your life today. Where are you incapacitated in loving God or yourself or another? Where do you need healing in your life? Respond. (*Pause.*)

"Now think of the father. Like him, you may have belief and unbelief in God's ability to heal you today. Focus on your openness to the possibility of God's healing you. Acknowledge your uncertainties and doubts. Then, if you can, like the father, ask for an increase in faith. Respond. (*Pause.*)

"Again, like the father, how can you act on your belief and bring your hurt to God for healing? Respond. (*Pause.*)

"At this moment imagine that a relative or a friend is bringing you, like the incapacitated boy, to Jesus for help. Visualize Jesus with you now, ordering the destructive spirits out of you, calming and restoring you, then lifting you up and setting you on your own feet. Take time to let this happen. Move into that experience with Jesus in any way that is helpful. Respond. (*Note to reader: use more time for silence here.*)

"Slowly, when you are ready, open your eyes and return your awareness to the room. If you want to make an entry in your journal, take time to do so."

E. Closing, Large Group (*ten minutes*)

Choose one or two of the following suggestions as appropriate for your group: evaluation of the session, song, details of next session, prayer in pairs, which might include the blessing, "Jesus desires your wholeness, and I do, too," or something similar.

INDIVIDUAL WORK

Purpose: To continue to be open to the healing and liberating work of Jesus in our own lives, in our relationships with others, and in the world.

1.   Read the story of the healing of the paralytic in Luke 5:17–26. Notice that for Jesus, bodily healing and forgiveness of sins are intimately connected. List areas of your life where you feel you need forgiveness or healing, where you feel broken, hurt, unfree, stuck, or paralyzed.

2.   Jesus taught that freedom and healing come when we share his outlook and activity, when we are instrumental in healing and freeing others. Jesus taught us to pray, "Forgive us the wrong we have done as we forgive those who wrong us" (Matt. 6:12, NAB). List as many people or situations as you can in which you sense there is something wrong in your relationship: estrangement, distance, feeling offended, hurt.

3.   The proclamation of "the acceptable year of the Lord" in Jesus' mission statement referred to the "year of the jubilee" (also mentioned in Lev. 25:8–55), a time when "the liberation of all the inhabitants of the land" was to be proclaimed and realized. Con-

sider proclaiming your own jubilee year by forgiving all the people you have just listed, letting them off the hook completely. It may help to picture them as doing the best they could given their circumstances.

4. Reflect on how this free act of forgiveness affects your own areas of paralysis and unfreedom mentioned in response to the first question.

5. Continue the reflection begun in the session on how your own transformation and your concern for social transformation are interwoven in your life. Are there changes you want to make?

6. *To prepare for the next session:* Write a brief summary of your personal work with the assignment.

Note: The theme of healing and cleansing is given further consideration in *Journeying with the Spirit*, Session 4.

SESSION 3

Friend/Mystery

Pascal wrote that we each have an empty spot in our heart that only God can fill. Years ago, as a lonely student in Scotland, I (Jackie) caught a glimmer of the truth of that statement. Naturally an outgoing person, I found it hard to face the fact that I had few friends on whom to rely for companionship and stimulation.

At the same time I had been on a spiritual quest. The basic foundation of the Christian faith made intellectual and ethical sense to me. The Bible was somewhat familiar. Church participation had been engaging. Yet, I sensed there was something more.

People I respected talked about prayer as our vital link to God and that a personal relationship with Jesus opened the channel to God. I was both attracted and resistant. These people, living from a quiet powerful center, had an irresistible appeal for me. Yet, others had accosted me with questions about whether I had been saved. The effect was to make me wary of anything that could be described as "a personal relationship."

One book drew me like a magnet. By Leslie Weatherhead, British Methodist pastor and counselor, *The Transforming Friendship*[1] put forward this message: what transformed the disciples was the experience of being with Jesus as friend. This friendship was a gift. It is available to us today just as surely as it was to Jesus' first friends. "Our attitude to a gift is acceptance," wrote Weatherhead. We do not have to understand it, struggle for it, or behave in a certain manner to warrant it.

Simply imagine or "*pretend* that it is true; and then you will find in your own experience how true it is, and imagination will grow up into faith," wrote Weatherhead. He added,

The way of argument is irrelevant and impossible. The way of experience is certain. Try it. Sit down quietly for ten minutes every day for a month. Let your mind go out to Jesus. Think about Him. Believe that what He once was He eternally is. What He was for men and women years ago, He is for you today. All His followers would guarantee that you will find Him no ghost, but a Friend; no mere memory of long ago, but a living personal Saviour whose friendship will transform your whole nature.[2]

When I tried Weatherhead's experiment of the imagination, I became aware of the presence of Jesus in a new way. As I walked alone in our Scottish village, it was as if Jesus were beside me. Being aware of that caused me to see the children playing in a way I had not experienced before. It was as if they and we were bathed in light and love, that we were one, that we were wrapped in a holiness that was truly wonderful.

I began to understand more clearly how Jesus taught his disciples. He did not give them books to read or rules to follow. He invited them to walk, talk, work, and be with him. His presence, his friendship, transformed people and situations in ways that words cannot fully capture. No wonder the Bible had not made more sense to me; I had confined Jesus to the prison of mere words. Now, for the first time, I moved beyond words and related to Jesus through the imagination. It had a noticeable effect. As Weatherhead had said it would, experience verified the power of this experiment. I came to experience a loving relationship with one who accepts us as we are but empowers us to be more.

When we experience God's love given freely, we are challenged to embrace others with compassion, particularly the needy and oppressed. "I was hungry and you gave me food. I was thirsty and you gave me drink. I was away from home and you gave me welcome" (Matt. 25:35, NAB). When these words are understood in the context of the love of Jesus, they take on new light. Most of us have a loved one for whom we would do anything, give our time, our energy, our very selves. "He's not heavy, he's my brother," reads the poster showing a young man carrying a younger brother. Love gives us energy and purpose with which to perform the difficult, the unappealing. That seems to be what St. Paul experienced when he said, "The very spring of our actions is the love of Christ" (2 Cor. 5:14, Phillips).

How do we experience this love? There are different ways, depending on temperament, circumstances, and background. Some experience this love by relating to God as friend, lover, companion, or parent. For them, prayer is like being with a loved one—talking, listening, being silent, or engaging in work or play.

Others find this sort of intimacy at odds with their concept of God as *mystery*. For them, prayer is real and effective but may take the form of walking in the woods, listening to music, or reading poetry. Ralph Keifer, professor of liturgical studies at Notre Dame University, writes that the vocation of those who experience God in this way "is to live before God as mystery, not as friend; or, more accurately perhaps, they are called to befriend the mystery that haunts them."[3] He says:

> Part of the experience of this spirituality of mystery is an intense intuition of there being something elusive, haunting, indirect, yet utterly compelling about which life relentlessly revolves. There is a sense of being drawn or pursued by something that is never quite tangible, that never quite allows any sense of a face-to-face meeting.[4]

Those who approach God this way have a sense of God's being positively involved in their lives and in the world, sustaining them but remaining intangible and mysterious. They acknowledge God's being as ultimately loving, supportive, calling them forth into deeper involvement with God and the world.

How can God or Jesus as friend and mystery live in us? Irene Claremont de Castillejo, English Jungian analyst, writes that enlivening experiences of love cannot be programmed. Love visits us. There are, however, ways we can position ourselves to welcome and recognize love when it knocks on our door.[5]

First, we can *open ourselves to it by naming our hunger*. This may be experienced as an inner emptiness, a search for meaning, or a longing for personal experience of God's presence. We can acknowledge that we want the powerful presence of love in our lives. That we have an inner emptiness which friends, family, work, and avocations cannot fill. That we are hungry not only for knowledge of God but for experience with God. That we seek meaning, purpose, companionship, compassion, empowerment from outside ourselves.

Then we can take a fresh *look at the facts about Jesus*. Many of us have not done that as adults. The picture of Jesus we have received from others may have turned us off. Jesus may have been presented as a stern taskmaster demanding allegiance or as someone meek and mild we would not want to know. Even our reading of the Bible may not convey a picture of Jesus we can relate to. A product of an ancient culture, it requires knowledge of that culture to understand. Biblical analogies from rural life may not be grasped by those unacquainted with that life. Portraits of Jesus have been put forward to support points of view that do not make sense to us. If we have had difficulty with our own father or brother, God seen as father or Jesus as brother may be loaded inappropriately with emotional baggage.

Help may come by turning to a reliable contemporary portrait of Jesus drawn by a respected biblical scholar. An example is *Jesus*

Before Christianity by Albert Nolan, provincial superior of the Dominican Order in Southern Africa. What emerges from Nolan's study is a man of remarkable compassion who believed that the structures of evil and sin could be overcome by the power of love. Nolan writes:

> When one allows Jesus to speak for himself . . . what begins to emerge is a man of extraordinary independence, immense courage and unparalleled authenticity—a man whose insight defies explanation.[6]

The Jesus whom Nolan found was a man of such good spirit that people sought him out and wanted to be in his presence. Moreover, he wanted to be with them and frequently invited them to dinner. As Nolan writes:

> It would be impossible to overestimate the impact these meals must have had upon the poor and the sinners. By accepting them as friends and equals Jesus had taken away their shame, humiliation and guilt. By showing them that they mattered to him as people he gave them a sense of dignity and released them from their captivity. . . . Moreover, because Jesus was looked upon as a man of God and a prophet, they would have interpreted his gesture of friendship as God's approval of them.[7]

Third, we can *say "yes" to Jesus' invitation to be with him*, even though we do not have all the facts. This profound but simple act produces a dramatic change of perspective. No longer seeing ourselves as outsiders, we now place ourselves within the circle of God's love. Evelyn Underhill, an English writer on the spiritual life, likens this change to entering a cathedral and viewing a stained-glass window from the inside with the light streaming through. The most wonderful scenes come alive. Before, from the outside, the window was dark and lifeless.[8] Saying "yes" changes our identity from that of onlooker to friend.

Once within the cathedral we can sit on the sidelines or *spend time with people whose faith is attractive to us*. They are available to us through the written page but also through personal contact. Ken Unger, Ohio pastor and writer, describes how loved by God he feels when a few people listen without judgment and accept him even when he is running away from God's call.[9]

Imagination makes God's presence real. Seeing its value much as Leslie Weatherhead did, Jean Houston, trained in theater and theology, describes Jesus' life as "high theater . . . a mystery play with ultimate and immediate human consequences."[10] We participate not by simply watching, but by taking our part in the drama. Houston writes:

> Acting "as if" you love God and are loved by God will prime the pump of your capacity for loving. . . . Your lack of belief in this can be bridged by the "as if." Your innate dramatic character will be engaged, and before too long you will discover that you truly do love the Beloved of your soul, and, from the abundance of this loving, you discover that you also love your fellow human beings.[11]

Teresa of Avila taught a method of prayer that engages the imagination in using scripture passages for reflection. First, read through the passage in order to see its sweep. Next, read it slowly and imagine the setting, the people involved, and the action. Try to enter into the scene, relate to the story in a personal way, and hear the words of Jesus spoken to you. Finally, ponder the significance of the scripture for your own life. Many Christians have used some form of this method in developing a deep awareness of the presence of Christ in their lives. (One such method is Karl Olsson's relational Bible study introduced in Session 3 of the first

book of the *Doorways* Series, *Encountering God in the Old Testament.*)

Finally, God's friendship can become real as we *cherish others*.
Frank Laubach, a pioneer in teaching illiterate adults to read,
knew this well. During his first year in the Philippines, he was very
much alone, learning the language of the Moros, a people among
whom he felt called to work. During that period he resolved to be
as open to God and to the needs of the people as possible. In his
diary, later published as *Letters by a Modern Mystic*, Dr. Laubach
describes the year as "a succession of marvelous experiences of the
friendship of God." How does this friendship develop? "Precisely
as any friendship is achieved. By doing things together. The depth
and intensity of the friendship will depend upon the variety and
extent of the things we do and enjoy together." He goes on to describe how God's friendship became a reality:

> All I have said is mere words, until one sets out helping
> God right wrongs, helping God help the helpless, loving
> and talking it over with God. Then there comes a great
> sense of the close-up, warm, intimate heart of reality.
> God simply creeps in and you *know* [God] is here in your
> heart. [God] has become your friend by working along
> with you. So if anybody were to ask me how to find God
> I should say at once, hunt out the deepest need you can
> find and forget all about your own comfort while you try
> to meet that need. Talk to God about it, and—[God]
> will be there. You will know it.[12]

To say "yes" to the love of God we see in Jesus means to align
ourselves with his purpose, to avail ourselves of a spiritual power
that activates our own, and to be open to a presence—whether of
mystery or friend—that we can know and love more deeply by
reaching out to those in real need.

GROUP DESIGN

Purpose: To open ourselves to a more intimate relationship with Jesus as friend and as mystery.

A. Gathering Time, Large Group (*ten minutes*)

Begin in a way that involves everyone, including any who were absent. Use a song, moment of silence, or perhaps share briefly how you are feeling as you come to this session.

B. Sharing Groups (*twenty minutes*)

Describe briefly one or two concrete ways you dealt with the Individual Work for Session 2 and in what ways you are open to the healing and liberating work of Jesus in your own life and with others.

C. Discussion of the Session Text (*thirty-five minutes*)

1. As you read the descriptions of those who relate to God most readily as friend or as mystery, which description do you identify with? Or are there other ways you would describe your response to God's love as expressed through Jesus?

2. The way others perceive and respond to God's love can expand our own relationship with God. As you hear how others respond differently from you, can you consider expanding your response? How? Give examples.

D. Experiencing Jesus as Friend/Mystery (*forty-five minutes*)

The session text includes six ways of becoming more intimately related to Jesus as friend or as mystery. They are:

✤ open ourselves to it by naming our spiritual hunger;

✤ look at the facts about Jesus;

✤ say "yes" to Jesus' invitation to be with him;

✤ immerse ourselves with people whose faith is attractive to us;

✤ imagine God's loving involvement in our lives and those of others;

✤ cherish others.

Take about fifteen minutes to write your reflections on the following questions:

1.   Am I open to a deeper relationship with Jesus as friend or mystery?

2.   Which of the steps mentioned above have I taken?

3.   Are there steps (mentioned or others) I should take in order to deepen this relationship?

After you finish writing, pair up with another and share your reflections as you wish. Writing and then speaking our clarities or confusions can often move us to a new place. Respond to one another with encouragement and/or prayer (fifteen minutes).

Use the remainder of your time (fifteen minutes) for a group reflection on the insights that may have occurred or on the difficulties encountered through your journaling and sharing.

E. Closing, Large Group (*ten minutes*)

Choose one or two of the following suggestions as appropriate for your group: evaluation of the session, song, details of next session, prayer.

INDIVIDUAL WORK

Purpose: To gain a biblical overview of Jesus as friend, to open ourselves to God's befriending of us in our needy areas, and to consider how we extend God's love to others.

1. Read the Gospel of Mark, the earliest and shortest account of Jesus' life and work, taking note of how you see Jesus embodying God as friend. Make a special note of any newness you discover or any insights that evoke in you a fresh response to God's love. (*Note:* If possible, read through Mark at one sitting, much as you would read a novel. Choose a readable translation. Then in other periods during the week, review and ponder the reading you did. This may seem like a demanding suggestion, but most of our participants are glad they were challenged to do this.)

2. The psychiatrist C. G. Jung felt that the key to healing the world and making it a place of compassion was to identify those parts of our inner world that we reject, then to befriend those parts and allow God to love them as well. Our groups have found the following passage from Jung helpful:

> If the doctor wishes to help a human being he must be able to accept him as he is. And he can do this in reality only when he has already seen and accepted himself as he is.
>
> Perhaps this sounds very simple, but simple things are always the most difficult. In actual life it requires the greatest discipline to be simple, the acceptance of oneself is the essence of the moral problem and the epitome of a whole outlook upon life. That I feed the hungry, that I forgive an insult, that I love my enemy in the name of Christ—all these are undoubtedly great virtues. What I do unto the least of my brethren, that I do unto

Christ. But what if I should discover that the least among them all, the poorest of all the beggars, the most impudent of all the offenders, the very enemy himself—that these are all within me, and that I myself stand in need of the alms of my own kindness—that I myself am the enemy that must be loved—what then? As a rule, the Christian's attitude is then reversed; there is no longer any question of love or long-suffering; we say to the brother within us "Raca," and condemn and rage against ourselves. We hide from the world; we refuse to admit ever having met this least among the lowly in ourselves. Had it been God . . . who drew near to us in this despicable form, we should have denied God a thousand times, before a single cock had crowed.[13]

Identify and practice ways to do what Jung suggests in this passage. Perhaps you can visualize an area of your life or a trait that you find unacceptable. Can you then visualize yourself in Jesus' company befriending this enemy within?

3.   Ponder the quotation from Frank Laubach in the text: "So if anybody were to ask me how to find God, I should say at once, hunt out the deepest need you can find and forget all about your own comfort while you try to meet that need. . . ." Focus on one way you could try that out this week. Record in your journal what you did and how you felt about it.

4.   *To prepare for the next session:* Write a brief summary of your personal work with the assignment.

SESSION 4

Teacher/Guide

"Is the universe friendly?" According to Albert Einstein, this is a central question for humanity.

The answer given by Jesus through his life and words is a resounding yes! At the core of the universe, he taught, is a heart of love—the embrace of God. God is here, now, totally for us regardless of our intelligence, background, class. God reaches toward us in love, wanting us to immerse ourselves in this love and extend it to others. God is available as guide to teach us how to live in that love. But God also reminds and challenges us when we fail to express this love.

This session invites us to ponder these teachings and to allow their power to guide our lives.

One of the most universally believed truths about Jesus is that he was a great teacher. Although not formally trained, he often was called "teacher" or "rabbi" in his day. Even today it is not uncommon to hear, "I don't know if he was God, but I do believe he was a great teacher."

Teaching occupied a substantial part of Jesus' ministry. As he inaugurated a new order of living and invited people to participate, he offered basic training in the new way. If the essence of good teaching is "Show, don't tell," Jesus showed by what he did and what he said.

The major way Jesus taught about God was how he lived. Rooted deeply in divine love, he identified with those who were unacceptable in his day—foreigners, women, sick people, corrupt officials. His aim was to awaken people's compassion for one another and to spark belief that people could live together in a just way. He went about healing, forgiving, speaking truth from his heart, demonstrating God's mercy especially in the face of resistance and opposition.

He usually taught with pictures, vivid sayings, and stories that caused people to see situations afresh and think for themselves. God's love reaches toward us, he said, like a shepherd looking for a lost sheep or a father running toward a wayward child finally returning home. We are to be connected to God's love, like branches growing out of a living vine. It is then that we will bear fruit, reaching to others in love as Jesus did.

The principle of overflow is introduced here. We are so fed, healed, and empowered by God's love that this love overflows in compassion for others.

Jesus shows us how to be nourished by this love. The Bible portrays him as seeking time alone in prayer. His public life began with forty days of solitude. Once his life in community began, he took time off by himself, stealing away to commune with God. So deep was this communion that Jesus conveyed an immediate sense of God's presence to others. They sought him out for healing, discernment, wisdom. So we are invited to do the same—to abide in God's love, to notice with wonder how God clothes the lilies of the field, and to notice, as Mary did, that the one who is mighty, who gives strength to the weak, has done great things for us.

Henri Nouwen, writer and teacher, reminds us that the evangelist John describes unconditional and unlimited love as God's first love. "Let us love," he says, "because God loved us first" (1 John 4:19). Human caring can be seen as a second love, derived from the first love. Sometimes this human love clearly reflects God's first love, but at other times is "only a broken reflection of the first love."[1] Because we may have been wounded by this partial second love, we are tempted to doubt the validity of the first. That is why we must take time again and again to experience this first love directly, allowing Jesus and others who best reflect that love to heal wounds inflicted by that second love when it was misguided.

A young friend said, "I would like to believe in God. Then I would know I am not alone. I would like to have someone to lean on, to guide me." Jesus had an answer for that sort of wistfulness. Say "yes" to God as guide, reorder your life with God as center, then seek God's guidance, and it will become apparent. We are free to be onlookers, we are free to question, we are free to walk away. God never violates this freedom. When we freely and consciously turn to God, we recognize with Jesus that the realm of God is in our midst.

Jesus taught for decision and change. When people said "yes" to God's desire to be welcomed into their hearts, noticeable change occurred. The blind saw, the mute spoke, rich people shared their goods, fishermen changed their occupations. Direct experience of God's love empowered them to live the greatest of Jesus' teachings, to love God in return with all their heart, soul, mind, and strength, and to love their neighbor as themselves.

If there was one thing Jesus preached against, it was hardheartedness. We see in the Gospel of Mark, for instance, his grief when people closed themselves off from God's healing and forgiving love. The contrast, for Jesus, was not softheartedness, but rather open-hearted acceptance of God's love and a wholehearted commitment to share that with others. It is then that the more demanding teachings of Jesus—that we suffer with those who suffer, that we allow God's forgiving love full sway in self and society even when confronted with death-dealing influences—are seen not as impossible burdens to avoid but as opportunities to witness to God's mercy.

To know the universe is friendly, to feel cherished and guided by love as Jesus did, to have that love pour out from us to others, to believe that society's structures can be transformed by love—is this farfetched? People bet their lives on these realities, embody this love, and make it real and tangible for us today. Their stories, methods, and language spark our efforts to do the same.

A physician called Dr. Rosen embodies the kind of reaching-out love we are talking about. John McGuire in *The Dance of Life* tells this story about Dr. Rosen's work in a New York hospital for mentally ill and seriously handicapped people.

> For the period during which he is going to work with a group of the most deeply disturbed patients, Dr. Rosen moves in on their ward, placing his bed right alongside of theirs. On the initial morning, having addressed a patient with "Good Morning" and having received no response—"surely he's aware," whispered the knowing nurses, "that that man hasn't spoken in ten years,"— Rosen suddenly strips off coat and shirt and tie and climbs directly into bed with the patient. He then begins the most intimate kind of mothering and love. He loves and embraces the patient again and again, wordlessly, employing only this primitive language of gesture that he is loved. Slowly, after varying periods of time, many patients are loved back into speech. Their first words are often "thank you, thank you."[2]

The Spanish word *cursillo* means "little course." The Cursillo Movement, started by a Spanish priest in the 1940s, gives participants firsthand experience of God's transforming love. About twenty people gather for a long weekend together. These are people specially invited by friends who have experienced God's love so deeply through Cursillo activity that they want to share it. These sponsors offer prayerful acts of support for their friends during the weekend. Another group of about ten serve as leaders for the event, meeting for weeks to prepare. The core experience participants describe, over and over, is of being loved by God and others in a gracious and unconditional way.

The ripple effect of these Cursillo weekends is impressive. In our area, small reunion groups of Cursillistas (weekend participants) meet regularly in homes, government offices, and places of business throughout the week. These people help one another re-experience God's first love and let it permeate their work and family life.

Shortly before his death, Jesus sat down for a meal with his disciples, now his intimate friends. Taking bread, he broke it and said, "This is my body broken for you. Take and eat." And pouring wine, "This is the cup of forgiveness, my blood poured out for you. Drink all of it." Through the ages, Christians have reenacted this meal as the Eucharist, or thanksgiving. There they receive an extension of God's love as embodied in Jesus. They allow themselves to be filled with God's first love.

Ernie Raskauskas is one who is frequently nourished by the Eucharist. The strength he receives from this and other dimensions of his faith flows over into his professional life. He has a unique opportunity to allow Jesus' teaching to influence societal structures. An American lawyer, he works with the Lithuanian president and parliament, helping them craft a new constitution for its emerging democracy. Together they are laying the foundation for a new legal system and for a just and peaceful society.

During the 1940s and 1950s, a small group of Catholics in mid-America began what later was called the Christian Family Movement. Eager to apply Jesus' teachings in their homes and society, couples met together to apply a simple but profound process to their lives: Observe, Judge, Act. This involved three steps:

1. Get the facts.

2. Evaluate the new information.

3. Take action.

Meetings began with a short reflection on a Gospel passage, focusing on what it was saying today. The story of the Christian Family Movement written by Rose Marciano Lucey teems with tales of "CFMers" seeing problems, analyzing the situation, and taking action. Here is one:

> At a PTA meeting in Evanston, Illinois, John and Dorothy Drish heard a talk by the chaplain of Cook County Jail. Touched by the fact that men drift back into crime because they can't find jobs, these creative CFM leaders gathered friends and strangers to form the Citizens' Committee for Employment, which included key leaders of business, labor, government and social welfare groups. Greeted with skepticism, the committee grew to be a reforming agency in the Cook County Jail. Dorothy says, "If it hadn't been for CFM, we'd probably have looked at the prisoners' problems and said, 'Interesting, but what has it to do with us?'"[3]

Dorothee Sölle and other liberation theologians couch Jesus' teaching in fresh language. They listen to and speak with the poor and the powerful, the dispossessed and the affluent, in First and Third World countries. For them, living God's truth involves befriending and empowering the poor, the marginalized, the hurting. It means placing persons before profitability. They interpret teachings such as "blest are you poor; the reign of God is yours" (Luke 6:20, NAB) by pointing out that Jesus was not neutral but sided with the poor, the outcasts, the invisible ones. Sölle suggests that taking up the cross and following Jesus means:

breaking with neutrality;
making the invisible visible;
sharing a vision.[4]

Marian Wright Edelman of the Children's Defense Fund is doing just that—lobbying for the rights of children, making their situation widely known, and sharing the dream that all children should be able to thrive. The Southern Poverty Law Center brings to public attention legal cases that need supplementary funding for justice to be served. Greenpeace makes visible environmental degradation so that all will take notice and do the hard work of envisioning an environmentally sound future.

These people apply Jesus' teaching of compassion to social structures. Quietly, others live it in personal ways. Ina Eaton cheerfully cares for her husband, George, now incapacitated by a stroke. Sally and Bob Dowling keep the support going to their learning-disabled son, Rick, so that he can attain the best education of which he is capable. Valerie and Dale Vesser invite Valerie's Aunt Pym to spend her last days with them.

Fresh language and interesting stories of people who take Jesus' teachings seriously open up the transforming power of those teachings. In the end, however, it is when we experience them working in our own lives that real growth occurs. We (Rhoda and Jackie) had often read Jesus' words about being reconciled with those from whom we are estranged before coming before God. A few years ago, we found ourselves incapacitated by misunderstandings arising from our differing interpretation of shared experiences. Finally, we decided to tackle our differences directly. Aided by conflict-management learnings, we identified each hurtful incident, said how it made us feel, and listened to one another with respect. Then we constructed a composite picture of what had really happened. We began the process fearing that our collaboration was at an end, but by the time we were through, we had a new desire to work together. A creative flow of ideas came.

There is transforming power for people and society in the truths Jesus taught. Why are they not taken seriously more often? They have the potential to unleash enormous creativity and compassion, so much needed today. The observation rings true: it is not that Christianity does not work; it has not been tried.

Jesus' teachings are not easy. They are full of paradox: simple and complex, comforting and confronting, compelling and freeing. They are open to endless misinterpretation and abuse. People are tempted to absolutize specifics when Jesus intended to stimulate thought and love. Some confuse the ideal of love with the contemporary wish to "feel good" or to "feel comfortable" about things.

Transformation and growth occur when, in response to God's first love, we are moved to love God, self, and neighbor. Jesus promised to guide us in making that love real after his death. We learn the essence of Jesus' teachings through getting to know Jesus well and through the stories of those who take Jesus seriously. Then, in our own lives, we can ask for specific guidance. To do this, we might pray questions like these.

✤ Who are the poor you want me to accompany?

✤ In what aspect of society do you want me to embody your compassion?

Listen in silence. Guidance may come in a deepened awareness of how to make God's love tangible.

In *The Divine Milieu*, Pierre Teilhard de Chardin, Jesuit paleontologist, prayed,

. . . compel us . . . to venture forth, resting upon You, into the uncharted ocean of charity.[5]

This is a beautiful description of God's undergirding love supporting us as we extend it to others.

GROUP DESIGN

Purpose: To evaluate sessions thus far, reflect on the qualities of a good teacher and to share those teachings of Jesus that have been most transforming for us.

Materials: Newsprint, colored markers, bread, serving tray or plate, Bibles.

A. Gathering Time and Evaluation, Large Group (*thirty minutes*)

Gather in a way that is appropriate for your group. Then move into a brief period of taking stock of how you and the group are doing in the course. In the first session, you shared hopes about what might happen as a result of this course. Take a moment to recall how you stated your hopes. Now make a few notes about how these hopes are or are not being realized plus your reflections on this question:

What could you and/or the group do differently to enable you to realize your hopes more fully?

When you have finished your individual reflection, go around the circle sharing briefly one thing you appreciate about your experience and one idea for improvement that either you or the group could try.

B. Sharing Groups (*twenty minutes*)

Consider sharing your reactions to these questions based on the Individual Work for Session 3.

1. What new perception of Jesus as friend surfaced for you in your reading of Mark?

2. How did you respond to the quotation from Jung?

3. How did you choose to implement the Laubach quotation?

C. Teacher of the Year, Pairs and Then Large Group (*twenty-five minutes*)

1. *Ones:* Select one person in your life who has encouraged you to discover truths in a helpful way. Name that person your Teacher of the Year. Take a few minutes to depict this person on paper through a sketch or using colored markers or words.

2. *Pairs:* Then turn to someone you have not talked with, show your picture, and describe briefly why that person was important to you.

3. *Large Group:*

   a. Display your pictures.

   b. Share the qualities of the people you talked about. What made them special?

   c. When you have finished your group portrait of a good teacher, reflect on how many of these qualities may have been present in Jesus, who was known as an effective teacher. An awareness of his human qualities as teacher may shed light on some of Jesus' teachings.

D. Experiencing Jesus as Teacher/Guide (*thirty-five minutes*)

Breaking open the biblical word through sharing and breaking bread together have been common activities among Christians throughout history. Here is a chance to engage in these activities.

1. *Preparation:* In the center of the circle, place some bread that can easily be broken and shared in the group.

2. *Alone* (fifteen minutes): Take time to look at the Sermon on the Mount (Matt. 5–7) or other passages if you wish. Select one teaching that has made a difference in two situations:

✤ in your own life or another person's life;

✤ in society.

3. *Large Group* (twenty minutes): When you are ready, share your example with the group. Then break a piece of bread off the loaf, but leave it on the serving tray. If you have extra time, end with informal discussion of how to incorporate Jesus' teachings more fully into your lives.

E. Closing, Large Group (*ten minutes*)

In the circle around the table, each one take and eat one of the pieces of bread symbolizing Jesus as the bread of life, his teachings giving substance to life. Those who wish to do so may end the session with informal prayer.

INDIVIDUAL WORK

Purpose: To become conscious of persons who embody Jesus' teachings in memorable ways and to focus on practicing one of Jesus' teachings more fully.

1. List a few of the people you have read about or know personally who make some of Jesus' teachings alive and relevant for you. Select one to think about more carefully. Why does this person impress you? What do you find attractive about the person? Are there ways you would like to resemble that person? Write your reflections in your journal. Often the people we admire have qualities that are latent within us and could be developed. Becoming conscious of why we admire another can be a step toward finding and nurturing those qualities in ourselves.

2. Reread Matt. 5–7 and select one teaching you would like to concentrate on this week.

a. Bring the teaching alive by engaging your creativity:

✤ Paint the teaching.

✤ Set it to music.

✤ Express it in movement or dance.

b. Ponder how you can practice this more fully. Make regular entries in your journal about your attempts to embody this teaching.

3. Read "Practice Random Kindness and Senseless Acts of Beauty," which follows under number 4. This whimsical/serious piece may trigger your wild and crazy side. Consider carrying out a few acts of "guerrilla goodness" this week.

4. *To prepare for the next session:* Write a brief summary of your personal work with the assignment. Read the text for the session.

✤ Practice Random Kindness and ✤ Senseless Acts of Beauty

It's a crisp winter day in San Francisco. A woman in a red Honda, Christmas presents piled in the back, drives up to the Bay

Bridge tollbooth. "I'm paying for myself, and for the six cars be-hind me," she says with a smile, handing over seven commuter tickets.

One after another, the next six drivers arrive at the tollbooth, dollars in hand, only to be told, "Some lady up ahead already paid your fare. Have a nice day."

The woman in the Honda, it turned out, had read something in an index card taped to a friend's refrigerator: "Practice random kindness and senseless acts of beauty." The phrase seemed to leap out at her, and she copied it down.

Judy Foreman spotted the same phrase spray-painted on a warehouse wall a hundred miles from her home. When it stayed on her mind for days, she gave up and drove all the way back to copy it down. "I thought it was incredibly beautiful," she said, ex-plaining why she's taken to writing it at the bottom of all her let-ters, "like a message from above."

Her husband, Frank, liked the phrase so much that he put it up on the wall for his seventh graders, one of whom was the daughter of a local columnist. The columnist put it in the paper, admitting that, though she liked it, she didn't know where it came from or what it really meant. . . .

In Portland, Oregon, a man might plunk a coin into a stranger's meter just in time. In Patterson, New Jersey, a dozen people with pails and mops and tulip bulbs might descend on a run-down house and clean it from top to bottom while the frail el-derly owners look on, dazed and smiling. In Chicago, a teenage boy may be shoveling off the driveway when the impulse strikes. What the hell, nobody's looking, he thinks, and shovels the neighbor's driveway, too.

It's positive anarchy, disorder, a sweet disturbance.

Senseless acts of beauty spread: A man plants daffodils along the roadway, his shirt billowing in the breeze from passing cars. In Seattle, a man appoints himself a one-man vigilante sanitation service and roams the concrete hills collecting litter in a super-market cart. In Atlanta, a man scrubs graffiti from a green park bench.

They say you can't smile without cheering yourself up a little; likewise, you can't commit a random act of kindness without feeling as if your own troubles have been lightened if only because the world has become a slightly better place.

And you can't be a recipient without feeling a shock, a pleasant jolt. If you were one of those rush-hour drivers who found the bridge fare paid, who knows what you might have been inspired to do for someone else later? Wave someone on in the intersection? Smile at a tired clerk? Or something larger, greater? Like all revolutions, guerrilla goodness begins slowly, with a single act. Let it be yours.[6]

SESSION 5

Savior/Prophet

It has been said that at the center of everything lies the cross, the pivot of history, at once the symbol of the failure of Christ's way of love and the beginning of its ultimate triumph.

What does a statement like this mean? How can something that happened two thousand years ago affect people today? An outsider might say that the cross is a disgusting tribute to hatred and cruelty, the resurrection an unbelievable event that flies in the face of scientific research, and Pentecost a strange happening among distraught people unwilling to accept the death of their leader.

In this chapter, we take an inside view of these events with Peter, who through them experienced Jesus as prophet and savior. Then we focus on what this prophet and savior can mean to us.

The words *prophet* and *savior* deserve attention. The dictionary definition of *prophet* is proclaimer of a revelation. Not only does the prophet speak the truth in a historical situation, the prophet embodies a vision of what could be. Theologian Walter Brueggemann in *The Prophetic Imagination* says that the prophet brings public expression to the newness given by God in particular situations.[1]

Jesus, as prophet, showed the people of his time another way to live: by sharing possessions, siding with the oppressed, treating one another as equals, serving others, embodying goodness no matter how strong the forces of evil, practicing solidarity with all peoples no matter how different.

The Bible portrays Jesus as more than a prophet; he is also described as a *savior*. This has been understood in various ways by the biblical writers and Christian tradition: Jesus saves us by paying the penalty for our sins through his sacrificial death on the cross; demonstrating the self-giving love of God; liberating us from the power of evil; serving as moral example.

The word *savior* for many of us stirs up a variety of associations. If we believe we are successful in life, we may not feel we need to be saved from anything. Or if we have been confronted insensitively by someone asking whether we are saved, we may have been unable to take the question seriously.

However, if we ask ourselves this question, something powerful can happen. When we think about it deeply, we then recognize that by following Jesus, we are saved from piling up possessions (materialism and consumerism), from ignoring people oppressed by others or by structures (social myopia), from thinking we are somehow superior or more deserving than others (elitism), and from feeling hopeless in the face of evil (despair).

If we heed Jesus' call to compassion and justice, our response will probably deepen and change as various challenges confront us. The story of how Peter's response to Jesus evolved can illuminate our own path. Four distinct phases mark Peter's developing relationship with Jesus: his first commitment to following Jesus; his flight when Jesus was crucified; his forgiveness and healing by the risen Jesus; his empowerment by the Spirit to extend Jesus' ministry after Pentecost. Through these varied experiences, Jesus not only acted as prophet and savior to Peter but called forth the prophet and savior in Peter. We see how this happened in the unfolding events of their lives.

Commitment: When Jesus called the disciples to proclaim God's realm of compassion and justice, Peter willingly said "yes." He and the other disciples made quite a stir, healing, teaching, and extending compassion to those in need. Their following grew, particularly among those who felt like outcasts or failures. When

Jesus asked Peter, "Who do you say I am?," Peter was the first to proclaim Jesus the anointed One of God (Mark 8:29–30, JB).

Gradually, a deepening storm developed over the impact of Jesus' life and work. Acceptance of his early teaching and healing gave way to a divided response among his disciples, the crowds, and the authorities. Conflict and confrontation increased. Authorities questioned Jesus' interpretation of the Law and concluded that his healing power was of the devil. People in the crowd walked away when challenged with the demands of the new order. The disciples became bewildered at their lack of power and their leader's increasing unpopularity; arguments arose. When Peter tried to deflect Jesus from going to Jerusalem for a confrontation with authorities, Jesus likened him to Satan! The cost of allegiance to God's love in the face of hostility was frightening.

Crucifixion: Finally, events converged at the cross. Jesus had threatened the religious and political authorities, who could stand it no longer. The realm of compassion and justice Jesus proclaimed was in direct opposition to the domination maintained by the Romans over the Jews, and the religious officials over the people. His consistent attention to women, children, prisoners, and outcasts violated the mores of the time.

As the storm mounted, Peter assured Jesus of his loyalty only to have Jesus predict that Peter would deny him three times. When asked to pray with Jesus in the garden, Peter fell asleep. Later, Peter refused to admit knowing Jesus, whom he had loved so unabashedly only days before. Finally, Peter isolated himself from the disciples and fled, distraught and afraid. As Jesus was tried, sentenced, and executed, Peter was nowhere to be found.

Despair and faith converged within Jesus on the cross. Feeling forsaken, he continued to pray. Mocked and tortured, he asked

God to forgive his tormentors. Alone, except for Mary and her friends at the foot of the cross, he let go of his life, his cause, his loved ones.

Resurrection: Gradually Jesus' followers came together in fear and mourning. Imagine their bewilderment when three women burst in saying that Jesus was not dead but had risen and would meet them in Galilee. The disciples' response was disbelief. However, astonishing events began to happen. Jesus appeared to them at their meetings and on the road, gently instilling the belief that his presence and love were accessible to them at any time.

Asked by the risen Jesus three times, "Do you love me?," Peter responded, "You know I love you." A deep healing of his three denials took place (John 21:15–19, JB).

In one of his final appearances, Jesus promised his followers they would be baptized with the Spirit and given power. They were told to wait in Jerusalem to be "clothed with power from on high" (Luke 24:49, JB). Returning in joy to the upper room where they had been staying, they joined in "continuous prayer" (Acts 1:14, JB).

Pentecost: Luke vividly describes this Spirit outpouring. A mighty sound, fiery flames, and the power to communicate God's message in languages previously not known were tangible signs of a fresh power in the disciples. Peter explained what happened by quoting Joel, an Old Testament figure who had prophesied that God would pour the Spirit upon "all flesh." Then Peter insisted that it was through belief in Jesus that this Spirit would be conferred. They should decide to live for God and be baptized in Jesus' name, so that whatever was wrong in their lives could be forgiven. Then they would be given the power of the Spirit to live love as Jesus did. Luke describes the impressive result:

> Then those who welcomed his message were baptized,
> and on that day alone about three thousand souls were
> added to the number of disciples. (Acts 2:41, Phillips)

Thus begins the story of the young church in action, as told in
the Book of Acts. Even a cursory reading of this remarkable book
reveals an astounding change of mood and activity among the disciples. Afraid and defeated at the crucifixion, then hopeful but
uncertain during the resurrection appearances, they appear in this
account as confident preachers, effective healers, and power-filled
proclaimers of the Realm of God. As J. B. Phillips says in the introduction to his translation of Acts:

> It is a matter of sober historical fact that never before
> has any small body of ordinary people so moved the
> world that their enemies could say, with tears of rage in
> their eyes, that these [people] "have turned the world
> upside down!" (Acts 17:6).[2]

At Pentecost, new energy surged into Peter and the disciples.
Suddenly, they were catapulted into action. They boldly carried
on Jesus' ministry of healing, preaching, teaching, and challenging the authorities. They came together in new communities,
house churches, where caring and nourishment flourished as solid
bases for ministry. Seeing the wider implications of Jesus' vision,
Peter extended God's love beyond the Jewish community to the
Gentiles. Challenged by obstacles, unafraid of opposition, Peter
and the disciples were on fire with a message and a ministry.

His words to Jewish Christians scattered by persecution ring
with confidence in God's call:

> May you know more and more of God's grace and peace.
> . . . Thank God . . . that . . . we have been born again

into a life full of hope. . . . This means tremendous joy
to you . . . it happens to prove your faith, which is infi-
nitely more valuable than gold, and gold as you know,
even though it is ultimately perishable, must be purified
by fire. . . . You come to [God] as living stones to the im-
mensely valuable Living Stone. . . . [God] has called you
out of darkness into [God's] amazing light. (Excerpts
from 1 Peter 1–2, Phillips)

Through these experiences, Peter received gifts from Jesus as
savior and *prophet*. Jesus saved Peter from his vacillating commitment, forgave his weakness, reassured him that new life is possible
even after denial, and empowered him to use his whole experience and gifts to further God's realm.

In summarizing Peter's response to Jesus, John Haughey, Jesuit
scholar, says that Peter evolved from being an observer to becoming a follower, then a disciple (learner), then a friend, and finally
an apostle (one sent forth).[3]

To develop our response to God's call, we can allow Peter's
journey to illuminate our own.

Commitment: When we say "yes" to the fullness of life Jesus
offers, we are introduced to his way of commitment and compassion. In this initial response, there may be many ups and downs,
times of understanding and bewilderment, efforts that are effective or that fail. We throw ourselves into serving others but may
get carried away, not unlike Peter, who tried to do everything. Initial enthusiasm may give way to weariness and disappointment.

Sometimes our initial response is ambiguous. We are aware of
other spiritual paths that have value. Here the experience of the
eighteenth-century French philosopher, René Descartes, is helpful. His life was devoted to the search for absolute truth. To do
this, he considered as openly as possible all sorts of observable ev-

idence. Realizing this search would take a lifetime, he wanted at the same time to be a practicing member of the Roman Catholic Church.

It is possible to put our full weight down in one spiritual tradition while remaining open to wisdom from other paths. The commitment phase of Peter's development challenges us to ask, "Where will I put my weight down? What is my response to Jesus' invitation to follow him, to live as he did?"

Crucifixion: There may come a time when we feel abandoned or forsaken in our commitment as did Jesus. And, like Peter, we may absent ourselves from contact with Jesus and his friends. A variety of factors can cause us to respond like this. Friends let us down; the Christian community fails in love or justice; a dear one dies cruelly; we become exhausted by taking on too much without sufficient support. This can cause us to be disappointed in God, self, or others. We are tempted to abandon our commitment as did Peter. Disillusioned, we quietly withdraw from our faith community without saying what is really in our hearts. Or we remain, but as frustrated, pessimistic people. We are in a "death place" and see no hope in others or ourselves. If this is where you are, can you give voice to your disillusionment and hurt?

No one has written more poignantly on this condition than sixteenth-century Spanish mystic John of the Cross. Our initial commitment to God's love may bring satisfaction and joy, which then are in danger of becoming conditions we require to feed our souls. At some point, these no longer suffice, and we begin to doubt God's love. We are thrown into what John calls "a dark night of the soul." Actually, according to John, this is God beckoning us to give up our attachments to relationships and possessions (no matter how spiritual or lofty) and inviting us to rely solely on God.

In *When Gods Die: An Introduction to John of the Cross*, Carmelite John Welch says that by means of "the night," God invites us to reorder our many loves by the deeper and more powerful love of God. By slowly accepting an invitation to a deeper love, we choose the path of "unpossessing and unknowing," the way of nothingness. As we travel this path of mystery, we are "supported by a Presence which, paradoxically, is most palpable when we have no resources left to continue the journey.

In "the night" experience, the soul softens. Welch writes:

> God is met as mystery; reverence replaces presumption. The soul conforms to the first commandment: "Have one God." . . . With a relationship to the true center of its existence, the personality begins to heal and function harmoniously. Other people are now not competitors nor extensions of ourselves, but are respected in their uniqueness.[4]

If we find ourselves in a "dark night," we can ask, "What is it, God, that you are trying to say to me? What idols have deflected me from anchoring myself firmly in your love?"

Resurrection: Encountering God through the darkness may help us, like Peter, to experience God's healing more deeply. This may reawaken our conviction that God is not absent or dead but alive and available. Wonder and hope revive. Like the disciples, we sense there is more to come and are waiting to see what it is.

Then it may be good to give voice to our hope while taking care that it does not harden into expectation. Psychiatrist Gerald May, in *The Awakened Heart*, contrasts the two: " . . . hope is a wish for something; expectation is assuming it is actually going to happen."[5]

He continues, "Real desire, the deeper prompting of our hearts, is where hope finds its continual beginning." May suggests that we "chip through our expectations to find our real desire" and that we "embrace our hope and lift it in consecration," that is, offer it to God for God's working out.[6]

If we find ourselves in a resurrection time, we may wait in patient reliance on God's timing for the next step in our journey to be revealed. And we may want to ask ourselves, "For what do I hope?" or "What is my deepest desire?" and then pray about the answers that come.

Pentecost: To Peter and the disciples, Jesus promised the gift of the very Spirit that resided in him. They were to go to Jerusalem and wait. By regrouping in the upper room where they had last shared a meal together with Jesus, and by being in "continuous prayer," they, in effect, brought their initial commitment to Jesus to a much deeper level. No longer reliant on his physical presence and leadership, they allowed his Spirit to pour into them and then acted out of that Spirit guidance and power.

Their experience triggers questions in us: "Have I opened myself to an outpouring of the Spirit? Aware of the forces that might have weakened initial commitment, have I said 'yes' in a more total way to the Spirit? In what ways do I experience the Spirit as awakener, comforter, guide, power?"

Saying "yes" to the Spirit places us in a new realm. We may be tested by the fire of doubt, despair, isolation, but we emerge not only trusting the creative Spirit but also more keenly touched by the world's pain. We become more mature carriers of God's healing, teaching, mercy, and justice.

Deciding to place our faith in God takes many forms. For some it may seem like a peak moment, when we are confronted by a chance to be radically open to God, to say "yes" more fully, perhaps, than ever before.

Such a time occurred to me (Rhoda) when I had gone through a period of increasing doubts about the goodness of God, or if God even existed. The slide down the slippery slope began slowly and picked up momentum as the months went by. Finally the day arrived when I was confronted by my inner emptiness while listening to several friends sharing their own faith stories. Later, alone, I dared to acknowledge my unbelief and saw my life stretch before me like a gray wasteland, without meaning or purpose.

In that moment I realized that I could do nothing to recapture my childhood faith or manufacture a new one. From somewhere inside me a cry for help seemed to form. I found myself whispering, "O God, if there is a God, I need you." Several minutes later, the silence became full of a presence that seemed palpable, a comforting, guiding presence that was utterly trustworthy and totally loving. This lasted for days and was followed by months of change and opportunities for growth.

The decision to trust God in this case took the form of letting go, admitting the truth of my need and calling for help. It led to a sense of Jesus' presence that was more immediate than ever before.

At the other end of the spectrum are situations in which growth is steady, slow, and undramatic. Brother David Steindl-Rast, Benedictine monk, describes it this way:

> Some people have peak experiences that are "big bangs" and some never have those but have a very strong, deep, slowly growing awareness that is a groundswell, that leads to a great sense of belonging.[7]

For those whose growth is gradual, affirmative decisions may look unspectacular and often take the form of a "yes" to keeping on the path, to remaining open and trusting. The person chooses to do the loving thing, to live with concern for others, for the world. Such a life may seem quite ordinary, but with all its ordinariness, there is power and purpose that points to something beyond simply human effort. There is a sense of a Spirit beneath the human spirit bringing fruitful action with far-reaching effects.

The phases of commitment experienced by Peter and by us are not like the rungs of a ladder on which we steadily climb to mature faith. They are more like threads that weave in and out of life in unexpected ways. They do not always happen in the same sequence as Peter's did. We may already be acquainted with the Spirit but then come to a place of crucifixion. Or we may come to initial commitment to Jesus and feel the Spirit flooding in at the same time.

In order and in details, these experiences vary. Throughout history, however, people have found deep resonance with the commitment/crucifixion/resurrection/Pentecost experiences of Jesus, Peter, and the other disciples. As we allow ourselves to be touched by these experiences, we become more open to the fullness of God's power to transform.

GROUP DESIGN

Purpose: To relive Peter's experience with Jesus and to allow it to touch us personally.

Materials: Bibles.

A. Gathering Time, Large Group (*fifteen minutes*)

Get everyone involved in a way that seems appropriate for this session.

B. Sharing Group (*twenty-five minutes*)

1. Share your response to item 2 in the Individual Work for Session 4. Which teaching did you choose, and how did you work with it?
2. Talk about your acts of "guerrilla goodness."

C. Walking in Peter's Shoes, Large Group (*sixty-five minutes*)

One of the members of our community, Mildred Allen, made a private silent retreat, taking only her Bible and a notebook. Moved to read the Gospel of Mark, she became fascinated with Peter's experience and found herself writing a journal from the viewpoint of Peter as he is portrayed in that Gospel. Putting herself in his shoes was a powerful experience. In this session, we join her by reading excerpts from "An Imaginary Journal of Peter" as she wrote it, then by studying crucial passages involving Peter, and finally by writing our own continuation of his journal.

1. Ask one person to read aloud the excerpts from "An Imaginary Journal of Peter," found after section D, Closing. (This takes about fifteen minutes.)
2. After listening to "Peter's journal," divide into four small groups. Assign each group one of the following passages: Peter's denial (Luke 22:54–62); empty tomb (Luke 24:1–12); after resurrection (John 21:1–19); after Pentecost (Acts 4:1–22).

    a. In your small group, choose one person to be a recorder/journalist who will write the continuation of Peter's journal based on the group's discussion. The group does the thinking. The recorder simply writes it down in the first person as if Peter were speaking.

    b. Read the Scripture aloud or silently in your group. As you do so, attempt to stand in Peter's shoes, imagining his feelings and responses.

    c. Talk about your perception of how Peter thought, felt, and responded.

    d. Help the recorder/journalist record your perceptions in journal form. (Use about thirty to thirty-five minutes for this read/share/write process.)

    3. All come together. Have someone reread aloud the last paragraph of Peter's journal. Then have the recorder/journalist read the four journal sections in chronological order. Leave a little silence after each reading for assimilation and pondering. (This should take about fifteen minutes.)

D. Closing, Large Group (*fifteen minutes*)

    Choose one or two of the following suggestions as appropriate to your group: evaluation of session, song, prayer, discussion of details for next session.

✤ An Imaginary Journal of Peter Drawn ✤ from the Gospel of Mark

    "I'm Simon. I'm just an ordinary fisherman, but some extraordinary things have begun to happen to me, and I want to keep track of them.

    "The other day my brother Andrew and I were casting our nets from our boat not far from shore. We saw the Nazarene, Jesus, walking along the beach. We waved, and he called to us, 'Come with me.'

"Wonder of wonders, without a word we dropped our nets, pulled ashore, and went with him. What made me do that? Suddenly, Jesus' authority, the truth of him, took me over. I have a sense that all fulfillment is in following him. The 'Come with me' of Jesus was a command really, but it was so promising, so loving, without guile, that it seemed powerfully alluring. (*Pause.*)

"The past Sabbath day a number of us were together in the synagogue in Capernaum. Jesus stunned us all when he spoke to a shrieking man who cried out, 'Have you come to destroy us? I know who you are—The Holy One of God.' Jesus spoke—as if to something in the man—'Be silent and come out of him!' Nothing could counter his command. The man went into convulsions and then was quiet, free from this unclean spirit.

"We five went to my house after that synagogue episode—my brother, James, John, Jesus, and me. My wife's mother had been sick, and I told Jesus about her as we approached. He went directly to her, took her hand, and helped her out of bed. She wasn't sick at all. The fever left her, and she began fixing a meal! Amazing! I'm trying to figure out what's going on. It seems unnatural, but it's good—always good. (*Pause.*)

"Early this morning I woke up to discover that Jesus had left the house. Later we found him. Strange—he was all by himself in a lonely place, praying. When we told him everybody was looking for him, he said, 'Come along. I must do the same work in other towns of Galilee. That's what I'm supposed to do.' So off we went—a few of us staying with him, committed to helping him, and lots of curious stragglers, too, walking along.

"Jesus says over and over in the synagogues, 'The time is now. The Reign of God is at hand—repent—turn your life around. Believe the good news.' I hear this over and over, and I don't know what he means. The way he heals is showing me there's something available that I haven't known about. It's something wonderful and good. (*Pause.*)

"Jesus isn't particularly careful about the way he puts his ideas across. He irritates the authorities by keeping 'bad company,' eating with just anybody, and what's more, doing things on the Sabbath that have been forbidden by the religious laws. It bothers me the way he challenges the Pharisees and the fellows with all the learning. He could get all of us in trouble. (*Pause.*)

"We're up in the hill country and Jesus has made twelve of us feel a deep fraternity with him. He's appointed us to be his companions. He says he is going to send us out to 'proclaim the Gospel,' and he's going to 'commission' us to drive out devils like he does. I don't feel able to do these things, but he wouldn't expect me to do them if I couldn't. He's given me a new name—calls me Peter instead of Simon. That makes me feel that something fresh and new is happening to me. I think he knows me better than I know myself. (*Pause.*)

"How busy life is getting now! Jesus is sending us by twos, teaching us his style of ministry. We take nothing with us but a walking stick—no food, no money—depending upon households to provide our needs in the villages where we go. (*Pause.*)

"Yesterday Jesus was teaching a huge crowd. We suggested that he send them to nearby villages to buy some food because they'd be weak with hunger. 'Give them something to eat yourself,' he said. 'What! Feed five thousand people? There are only five loaves of bread and two fishes,' somebody reported. 'That won't go very far in this situation.' But Jesus told us to have people sit down on the ground. Before our eyes, he took the bread and fish in his hands, said a blessing, divided it, and gave the pieces to us to distribute. Can you believe it? Everybody had enough, and we had twelve basketfuls left over. How do you account for that? (*Pause.*)

"We're in a village in Caesarea Philippi. My spirits are so high I can hardly keep my feet on the ground. We've been telling Jesus that people are speculating that he is Elijah or some other reborn prophet. Jesus suddenly turned to me and asked, 'Who do you say that I am?' To my utter amazement, I fell to my knees and replied. 'You are the Messiah, the Son of the Living God!' It was as if something took me over. I could tell that Jesus was moved by my response. Now I know who he is! And he knows that I know. How can I contain it? (*Pause.*)

"Up so high one minute, down so low the next. Just when we are beginning to feel like an effective group under Jesus' leadership, he's begun to talk about being handed over to the authorities in Jerusalem—rejected, tormented, killed. I couldn't bear to hear this. When he finished talking, I took his arm and said, 'Don't talk like that. I can't stand it.' He turned to me, looked me in the eye and said, 'Away with you, Satan! You think as a human being, not as God thinks!'

"That shut me up. Yet how can I imagine this man whom I love, the one I've watched for over two and a half years doing astonishing works for good, put to death by powers that are afraid of him? How can I bear to let the hope of Israel be overcome by evil schemers?

"He says plainly something I almost missed in my burst of temper: three days after his death he'll rise again. I've seen him bring the dead alive. I've seen it. But why does he have to suffer? It's terrible. It isn't right. (*Pause.*)

"I can scarcely believe what's happened. Yet I was there. Jesus chose me and James and John to go with him up a high mountain. We were alone there, we four, and suddenly before our eyes Jesus was transfigured. His clothes became dazzling white, and then two figures appeared talking with him: Elijah and Moses. I was so amazed I blurted out, 'O Jesus, it's so good to be here! Should we make three shelters for you?' I was so stunned that I was talking nonsense. But I was completely silenced by a voice that came from a cloud: 'This is my Son, my Beloved; listen to him.' And just as suddenly it all disappeared, and we were alone with Jesus. He told us not to mention what happened here until after he had risen from the dead. There it was again—that forecast. (*Pause*.)

"Another thing he has been saying is 'If anyone wants to be first, he must make himself last of all and servant of all.' (*Pause*.)

"What a day! My spirits are high. Jerusalem went wild over Jesus today, shouting and yelling and singing his praises. Of all things, he decided to ride on the colt of an ass to go into the city! We put our coats on the colt to make it look a bit more regal, and people threw flowers in his path all the way to the Temple. It was terribly exciting! He has gathered a lot of followers in these three years we've known him. When we finally reached the Temple, it was late in the day and we were all exhausted. (*Pause*.)

"Another day to remember! We walked to the Temple in the morning. I guess Jesus had had his fill of that scene the day before, because he went into furious action, driving out all the people who were buying and selling in the Temple. He upset tables and sent money and pigeons flying. Then he spent the day teaching from the Scriptures in a way that challenged the authorities. The priests were so furious they could have done away with him, but they were afraid, because he is so popular with the crowds. When evening came, we all left the city again. (*Pause*.)

"My brother Andrew and I and James and John had a private time with Jesus on the Mount of Olives, looking down on the Temple. We are confused about the way things are going and by what Jesus says is going to happen to him. Yet now I've become completely devoted to Jesus. I'd give my life for him! Still, I'm afraid of being put to the test. There's so much I don't understand. Why is he insisting on walking into trouble? But no matter what, I'll stand by him."

INDIVIDUAL WORK

Purpose: To use Peter's experiences as stimulus to becoming more conscious of where we are at this point in our own experience with God and what next steps are appropriate in our situation.

1. Reread and ponder "An Imaginary Journal of Peter" and the scripture passages used in the session, noting points that seem particularly relevant to you.

2. Reflect and do some writing on these questions:

> a. Considering the four periods—commitment, crucifixion, resurrection, Pentecost—which period is most descriptive of my life now? It may help to think of these periods as follows:
>
> ✤ Commitment—living with an openness and responsiveness to life
>
> ✤ Crucifixion—living with confusion, darkness, pain
>
> ✤ Resurrection—experiencing new hope, new life
>
> ✤ Pentecost—having a mature, tested commitment and sense of empowerment
>
> b. Do you sense an openness to another period? If yes, can you take steps to move into this different period?
>
> c. Contemplate Jesus as savior and prophet and your own life. What gifts are there for you?

3. *To prepare for the next session:* Write a brief summary of your personal work with the assignment. Read the text for the next session.

SESSION 6

Spirit/Presence

"Come, Holy Spirit, renew the whole creation." This short plea has become one of our favorite prayers. It was the theme of the Seventh Assembly of the World Council of the Churches which met in Canberra, Australia, in February 1991.[1]

The Canberra theme expresses some striking developments in the worldwide Christian community. In contrast to the theme of the previous assembly, held in Vancouver, "Jesus Christ, the Light of the World," Canberra's theme highlighted the importance of seeking wisdom together through prayer. Both assemblies featured aboriginal peoples as bearers of wisdom for all. The Canberra prayer, by addressing the Spirit, links Christian prayer with that of native religions, which also address the Spirit. In this way, the council affirmed the wisdom of these traditions. Furthermore, the Canberra theme includes the whole creation, not simply humanity, accenting our greater sensitivity to the interdependence of all creation.

"Come, Holy Spirit, renew the whole creation." How wonderful for this to be prayed in so many languages by so many different people! And how Earth-changing if all people would join in this prayer and embody it with an explosion of creation-renewing actions, local and global.

This session focuses on the Spirit's outpouring to the disciples, in subsequent history, and within us. It then invites us to open ourselves more fully to the Spirit's presence now and in the future.

An extraordinary promise was made by Jesus in his last conversation with the disciples,

"Truly, truly, I say to you, whoever believes in me will also do the works that I do; and greater works than these will they do, because I go to God." (John 14:12, Inclusive Language Lectionary, p. 157.)

As mentioned in the last chapter, at Pentecost an outpouring of the Spirit occurred with some striking signs, including the ability to make known in many languages the message of liberation. This immediately extended the range of the loving ministry of Jesus. The power of this outpouring was so compelling that a remarkable number of people became Jesus' followers: ". . . there were added that day about three thousand souls" (Acts 2:41, RSV).

Similar experiences of receiving the Spirit are recorded throughout the Book of Acts. This happened to the Samaritans (Acts 8:14–17), to Paul (Acts 9:1–19), and to the gentile Cornelius and his relatives and friends (Acts 10). As Jesus' followers tried to understand what was happening, they began to identify two elements of conversion: being baptized with water in the name of Jesus, and being baptized in the Holy Spirit. There seemed to be no set order to how this happened. What was essential, they realized, was receiving ever more fully the love offered by Jesus through the Spirit and then extending it ever more widely across boundaries that had not been crossed. This openness resulted in an outpouring of power, guidance, and confidence.

The lives of those who received the Spirit were marked by three common characteristics. First, they experienced *direct access to God through prayer* and felt guided by God even though Jesus was not physically present. They felt led by the Spirit in every dimension of life: what they said, what they did, where they went, how they acted. A striking example was when the Spirit guided the apostle Philip to pull alongside the chariot of an Ethiopian official who happened to be reading the words of Isaiah and who asked Philip their meaning. His reply was so convincing that the official asked to be baptized then and there (Acts 8:26–40).

In Corinth, when Paul's message threatened his hearers who "turned against him and abused him," he received these words from the Spirit in a vision:

> Do not be afraid, but go on speaking and let no one silence you, for I myself am with you and no one shall lift a finger to harm you. (Acts 18:9–10, Phillips)

Second, this direct access to God acounted for unusual *power and effectiveness in mission*. They preached boldly (Acts 9:29), healed all who came (Acts 5:15–16), confronted resistance with Spirit wisdom (Acts 6:10) and with unconquerable joy (Acts 5:41), and took their faith to cities and villages not reached by Jesus.

Third, for *mutual encouragement and support*, the early Christians met in small groups to share resources, break bread, pray, solve problems and differences, and plan for mission. Often they paired in ministry—Paul and Barnabas, Paul and Timothy, Priscilla and Aquila. Their calling was received directly from Jesus:

> You shall receive power when the Holy Spirit has come upon you; and you shall be my witnesses in Jerusalem and in all Judea and Samaria and to the end of the earth. (Acts 1:8, 9, RSV)

Their message rang out: God is in your midst. Center your lives in God's love. Be lovers of God, all people, yourself. Jesus is the Beloved of God. He is alive. Listen to him. The Spirit of God is revealed in you as you embody the same compassion and justice Jesus did. You will experience failure in your attempts to do this. But don't be discouraged. As you turn again to the God of love, you will be forgiven and empowered to begin afresh. Put God's justice and compassion before cultural and religious traditions. Let them be first in your life.

There is no doubt that something remarkable had happened. As John Haughey says in *The Conspiracy of God*,

> In an unprecedented way the active Power and Presence of God . . . erupted . . . in the human order.[2]

This unlikely band of believers extended Jesus' works of compassion and justice further than he was ever able to do when physically present.

Throughout history, the Spirit of God has continued to "be present in and course through the world by means of persons and communities."[3] They have further expanded Jesus' ministry, and enable us to do the same. Reflecting on these people and what they taught illuminates how the Spirit works in our lives. Several have been among our primary teachers.

The Quakers, through their founder, George Fox, and the contemporary writer, Thomas Kelly, remind us that everyone can have direct access to the Spirit and that the condition needed to attain this communion is an inner silence of the heart where God speaks.

In 1643, the Englishman George Fox began questing for a fuller life with God. Seeking help through the church members, clergy, and other "professors" of faith, he found "they did not possess what they professed." Profoundly disturbed by his own deep God-hunger and the mediocrity he found in himself and others, he was driven deep within for insight and guidance. He describes what happened:

> When all my hopes in [professors of faith] were gone, so that I had nothing outward to help, nor could I tell what

to do, then, O! then I heard a voice which said, "There is one, even Christ Jesus, that can speak to thy condition." And when I heard it my heart did leap for joy.[4]

What Fox did and urged others to do was to search through the Bible for the Spirit who had inspired the writers in the first place. Within Fox and his friends, there blossomed a power to spread the love of God and a clarity of vision that were to affect England dramatically. Other seekers had similar experiences of the Light of God within. Gradually they formed societies that became known as the Society of Friends. Their worship and faith practice were deceptively simple. Silently waiting alone and together for the Spirit to manifest itself, they were receptive to God's guidance. Marvelous things happened.

> A great light and spiritual power blazed out in England, beginning about 1650, which shook thousands of their complacent formalism, which kindled men and women with radiant fires of divine glory and holy joy. It sent them out into the market places and the churches, ablaze with the message of the greatness and the nearness of God, God's ready guidance and God's unfolding love. The blazing light illuminated the darkness, the shams, the silly externalities of conventional religion. It threw into sharp relief the social injustices, the underpaying of servants, the thoughtless luxuries, the sword as an instrument of social or "Christian" justice.[5]

Intentional communities have been another source of inspiration. Their members live a covenanted life witnessing to the Spirit's power focused on particular needs or possibilities. These have had a variety of manifestations, such as monastic orders like the Franciscans or communities like L'Arche (where mentally handicapped people live together). There is a power in a group of people committed to listen together for Spirit guidance. Particularly influential for us has been the Church of the Saviour, an ecumenical community in Washington, D.C., whose influence has been felt far beyond that city. It believes each one of us is called and gifted by God, and that the ways this is manifested are endless.

Also important for us is the Taizé Community in France. Founded in 1940 by Swiss pastor Roger Schutz, its call is to do something denominational parishes cannot do—embody the unity the Spirit gives. Composed of Protestants and Roman Catholics, this community cultivates a "passion for unity," a mission that has special resonance among young people and the dispossessed.[6]

Roger Shutz and his community have taught us that we can experience the richness of the Spirit by allowing the treasures of different traditions to commingle within each one of us. In our own Partners Community, we have been deeply enriched through trying out and incorporating practices learned from one another's faith communities.

In the sixteenth century, Teresa of Avila, tireless reformer of the Carmelites, showed that demanding vocational commitments can only be sustained by a rich inward life. Her work, *Interior Castle*, pictures every spiritual condition we are likely to experience as we seek to be faithful containers for the Spirit's presence.

Another Carmelite, Thérèse of Lisieux, who as a young person was unusually filled with God's love, lifted up "the little way" of celebrating the Spirit's presence in every circumstance of life, particularly the most ordinary and even the most irritating. Her world was small—her own convent in France during the late nineteenth century—but her vision was enormous: that everyone could know themselves to be cherished by God. Her tools seemed weak compared to her vocation to make God's love known to all: private prayer and personal writings in response to requests from others. But no one is more compelling in her invitation to celebrate the Spirit in everyone.

The materially poor remind us that it is to them that Jesus preached his liberating message. And as long as one person is poor, we all are poor. As we cooperate in systems that oppress people, we prevent the full presence of God in the world. Mexican Sister Adriana Mendez-Penate, who works with the poor struggling for a new society, told us, "It is not that we want you to live with the poor, but to take a conscious stand to act from the point of view of the poor." And Mary Cosby, a founder of the Church of the Savior, said, "Have one friend who is not in your economic class. Just be friends." As we do this we learn how possible it is to live with less and how essential is the wisdom of those who know how to do this.

Today spiritually aware men and women challenge us to embody mutuality, inclusivity, and interconnectedness—precious Spirit gifts—in everyday life. They urge us to know and be led by our own truth, and to listen with openness to the truth of others. This is a key doorway to spiritual maturity, according to Sherry Ruth Anderson and Patricia Hopkins. In *The Feminine Face of God,* they describe how breaking free of cultural or religious conditioning is a necessary step toward deeper, more personal awareness of the sacred in all life. Having interviewed women recognized for their spiritual maturity, Anderson and Hopkins conclude,

> If there is one thing we learned from women about their spiritual development, it is that clinging to ideals about how one ought to be blocks the gateway to mystery, while honoring what is personally true in each moment brings one into relationship with the sacred.[7]

As we share that deeper awareness in ever wider circles, we see our underlying commonality and learn to honor our differences.

The earth itself can be our teacher as it reveals the crying need for compassion for all creation. This cry must be heeded by every person if our grandchildren are to inhabit a healthy planet. Too many of us have been indifferent to this dimension of the Spirit's call. Now the Earth is telling us we have no choice. Planetary survival is at stake. Fortunately, more and more people are hearing this call and finding in the Bible and in other religious traditions the wisdom needed to care for the Earth.

Space scientist Carl Sagan recently authored "Preserving and Cherishing the Earth," an appeal sent by scientists to religious leaders calling for a joint commitment to preserve the Earth.[8] What will be required of everyone, he writes, is a vision of the whole Earth as a fragile, interconnected web of life that can thrive only if all of us learn to live simply and in tune with the processes of nature.

Each of us is called to play our part in renewing the whole creation. As we heal, forgive, and create pockets of health in our homes and in society, we do just that. Jesus was not able to plant trees, create schools, pass legislation, make cities work. As we bring the Spirit to these endeavors, we make real what he promised—greater works for the greater good (John 14:12).

Our tradition is replete with teachers ready to instruct us in the ways of the Spirit as we expand compassion and justice to all peoples. Never before has Spirit-living been so urgent. We invite you to join us in the prayer with which we began, three times for the Lover, the Beloved, and the Spirit of Love, and to hear and heed teachers who can help us back our prayer with action:

Come, Holy Spirit, renew the whole creation.
Come, Holy Spirit, renew the whole creation.
Come, Holy Spirit, renew the whole creation.

GROUP DESIGN

Purpose: To share how relating to Jesus through this course has affected us personally and to consider new ways of growth we might pursue as we leave the course.

Materials: Newsprint, marking pen.

A. Gathering Time, Large Group (*fifteen minutes*)

Get everyone involved in a way that seems appropriate for this last session.

B. Sharing Groups (*thirty minutes*)

Go around the group and share your responses to the three questions asked in the Individual Work for Session 5, number 2 a, b, and c). Use the time left for discussion and response.

C. Final Experience of Sharing, Large Group (*forty-five minutes*)

1. Place these questions on newsprint so all can see.

   ✦ In what ways has contact with Jesus through this course nourished your spirit? What questions and resistances remain for you?

   ✦ How did Peter's faith experience affect your own? In a few words, describe where you are at this point in your faith journey.

   ✦ What communities or persons have taught you about the Spirit? What have you learned?

✤ *Next steps:* Are there new ways of growth you want
to consider as you move from this course? Can you
describe them?

2. *Journaling:* Use fifteen minutes of silence for reflection
and writing on these questions.

3. *Large-group sharing:* For about thirty minutes, have a free
time of sharing feelings, insights, questions, perceptions of growth,
and appreciations.

D. Closing Celebration, Large Group
   (*thirty minutes*)

Devise a way to celebrate the ending of this course with
music, prayer, movement, refreshments.

INDIVIDUAL WORK

(For people who are working with this course by themselves)

Purpose: To reflect on how relating to Jesus through this course
has affected you personally and to consider new ways of growth
you might pursue.

1. Write your answers to the four questions asked in section
C of the Group Design.

2. Devise a way to symbolize what this course has meant for
you. You may want to do this alone, or with another person. Rit-
ualizing our current experience of seeking, questioning, growth,
even disappointments can give us a greater sense of our own inner
realities and a deeper respect for our spiritual journey.

NEXT STEPS

At this writing, our society and many people in it seem at a low ebb. Though heartening world events have occurred, individuals seem paralyzed by problems so huge as to be insoluble. According to New Testament scholar Albert Nolan, Jesus lived in a similar time when people felt hopeless nationally and personally.

Into this demoralized atmosphere came Jesus with an entirely different way and word. Claiming "to know the truth and to know it without having to rely upon any authority other than the truth itself,"[1] says Nolan, Jesus put forward that truth as something he chose to embody. His invitation to us is to embody it as well.

That truth, simply put, is that goodness can and will triumph over evil. Despite the structures of evil and the magnitude of its influence, there is a power that can overcome it, and that power is love. It is the heart of our relationship with God and the fuel that powers our reaching out to others.

At a critical juncture in his ministry, Jesus asked his disciples, "Who do you say that I am?" Peter was the first to recognize that Jesus was the anointed one of God.

In these chapters, we have had opportunity to answer the same question from different angles. Who is Jesus for me at this juncture in my life? And who is Jesus for society at this period? He is the one who, as a baby, reaches to our heart and offers healing, companionship, and guidance. He is the one who staked his life on the compassionate way and invites us to do the same.

When we accept his invitation, we become carriers of hope, creating islands of light in homes, businesses, schools, churches, and communities. In each of these situations we are invited to open ourselves to the loving "inflow of God," to use the words of John of the Cross. Commenting on what happens when we do this, John Welch writes:

> In the process our humanity is transformed. We begin to live from an interior place where our prayer is God's prayer, and our activity is God's activity.[2]

Thus, a fitting way to continue the work you have done in this book is to ask in every situation, "What is your prayer, God?", then to pray that, and "What is your activity?", and then to do that.

When Jesus invites us to follow him, to live as he did, to be carriers of the Spirit that filled him, he invites us to a process of ongoing conversion that continues throughout life. Gradually we open more of ourselves to the transforming power of God's love— our physical, emotional, mental, social, financial, and vocational selves.

This is not done in isolation. Rather, we are invited to join a people who for two thousand years have allowed God's love as revealed in Jesus to order and center their lives. To continue to explore the spiritual treasures discovered by this people, you might want to work with another book in the *Doorways* Series.

If you wish to meet the God described by the Hebrew people and known so well by Jesus, you might turn to the first volume, *Encountering God in the Old Testament*. To experience time-honored spiritual practices that strengthen our love of God, self, and others, consider *Journeying with the Spirit*. And if you are eager to discern which particular way you are called to share God's love with others, *Discovering Your Gifts, Vision, and Call* might be a good way to proceed.

To send you off, we conclude with a story that is worth pondering:

Abbot Lot came to Abbot Joseph and said: "Father, according as I am able, I keep my little rule, and my little fast, my prayer, meditation and contemplative silence; and according as I am able I strive to cleanse my heart of thoughts: now what more should I do?" The elder rose up in reply and stretched out his hands to heaven, and his fingers became like ten lamps of fire. He said, "Why not be totally changed into fire?"[3]

ADDITIONAL RESOURCES

For more on companionship with Jesus:
Pfeifer, Carl J. *Presences of Jesus*. Mystic, CT: Twenty-Third Publications, 1984. Beginning with the Gospels, this focuses on how Jesus is present today.
Underhill, Evelyn. *Light of Christ*. Wilton, CT: Morehouse-Barlow, 1982. Meditations on Jesus in the various stages of his life.
Weatherhead, Leslie D. *The Transforming Friendship*. Nashville, TN: Abingdon, 1977. How the friendship of Jesus can become real and powerful in our lives.

Wholeness and healing from various perspectives:
Bakken, Kenneth L., and Hofeller, Kathleen H. *The Journey Toward Wholeness: A Christ-Centered Approach to Health and Healing*. New York, NY: Crossroad Publishing, 1988. Based on biblical wisdom, this book combines spiritual, psychological, and physical factors in promoting health.
Brewi, Janice, and Brennan, Anne. *Mid-Life: Psychological and Spiritual Perspectives*. New York: Crossroad Publishing, 1982. The relevance of Jesus to people in midlife.
Stapleton, Ruth Carter. *The Gift of Inner Healing*. Waco, TX: Word Books, 1976. The healing of memories.
Welch, John. *When Gods Die*. Mahwah, NJ: Paulist Press, 1990. An introduction to John of the Cross. How God invites us to deeper response, which enables us to let go of lesser gods.

Communion with Jesus through prayer:
Carretto, Carlo. *Letters from the Desert*. London: Darton, Longman & Todd, 1972. Meditations from one of the Little

Brothers of Jesus, whose calling is to follow Jesus as literally as possible.

de Waal, Esther. *God Under My Roof*. Orleans, MA: Paraclete Press, 1985. Celtic prayers from island people who cultivated a consciousness of God through the activities of each moment of the day.

French, R. M., trans. *The Way of a Pilgrim*. San Francisco: HarperSanFrancisco, 1991. How a Russian pilgrim learned to be continually conscious of Jesus' presence.

Nouwen, Henri J. M. *Behold the Beauty of the Lord: Praying with Icons*. Notre Dame, IN: Ave Maria Press, 1987. How meditation on four Russian icons brings us into an immediate awareness of God. Includes reproductions of each icon.

Jesus and the Holy Spirit:

Haughey, John C. *The Conspiracy of God: The Holy Spirit in Us*. Garden City, NY: Image Books, Doubleday, 1976. The meaning of the Holy Spirit in our lives.

Jesus, justice, and ministry:

Brown, Robert McAfee. *Unexpected News*. Phildelphia: Westminster Press, 1984. How Third World Christians interpret the Bible.

Donders, Joseph G. *Risen Life, Healing a Broken World*. Maryknoll, NY: Orbis Books, 1990. Explores themes in Luke's Gospel and their relevance to current justice issues.

Gutierrez, Gustavo. *The Power of the Poor in History*. Maryknoll, NY: Orbis Books, 1983. How the poor see Jesus and apply his teachings today.

Nolan, Albert. *Jesus Before Christianity*. Maryknoll, NY: Orbis Books, 1978. This book's purpose is to "let Jesus speak for himself." It brings the reader to a fresh appreciation of who Jesus was in his time and shows how faith in Jesus equips us to be carriers of compassion in our time.

Nouwen, Henri J. M. *In the Name of Jesus*. New York: Crossroad Publishing, 1989. How relationship with Jesus forms us for ministry and leadership.

Sölle, Dorothee, and Steffensky, Fulbert. *Not Just Yes & Amen: Christians with a Cause*. Philadelphia: Fortress Press, 1985. A readable and engaging introduction to Jesus for people who want to live their faith in ways that challenge injustice, war, violence. Written for young people.

Wallis, Jim. *The Call to Conversion*. San Francisco: Harper & Row, 1983. Gives the biblical and historical meaning of conversion and its importance for the work of justice and peace.

Women and Jesus:
Moltmann-Wendel, Elisabeth. *The Women Around Jesus*. New York: Crossroad Publishing, 1982. Reading the stories of women in the Gospel with new eyes.

Ruether, Rosemary Radford. *Sexism and God-Talk*. Boston: Beacon Press, 1983. A feminist vision of Jesus, Mary, the Christian community, grace, shalom—in short, a fresh theology in the Christian context.

Schüssler Fiorenza, Elisabeth. *In Memory of Her*. New York: Crossroad Publishing, 1983. A feminist reconstruction of Christian origins, with particular emphasis on the image of God's realm as the festive meal that includes everyone as equals.

Wahlberg, Rachel Conrad. *Jesus According to a Woman*. New York: Paulist Press, 1979. Seeing through the prejudice that has blocked scriptural insights, and recovering much warmth and richness of the Gospel stories.

Further encounters with Jesus through the use of Scripture:
The Gospel in Art by the Peasants of Solentiname. Edited by Philip and Sally Scharper. Maryknoll, NY: Orbis Books,

1984. Reflections and artwork related to the Scriptures offered by the peasants of a community in Nicaragua.

Wink, Walter. *Transforming Bible Study*. Nashville, TN: Abingdon Press, 1980. Biblical stories come alive through the
process used in this book, bringing the reader to deeper personal insights.

If you have not used the other books in the *Doorways* Series, consider:

Encountering God in the Old Testament. To examine the question, "Who is God?" and to experience God as creator,
caller, deliverer, covenant-maker, suffering servant, and
new song. This offers a rich foundation for understanding
our spiritual roots.

Journeying with the Spirit. To experience practices that deepen
our relationship with the Spirit. These include healing, listening, and exploring God's presence over the span of our
lives.

Discovering Your Gifts, Vision, and Call. To explore our sense of
call and to relate that with God's vision and our gifts.

The *Doorways* Series, when offered in a parish, can be a catalyst
for change in individuals and in the congregation. To learn more
about how a parish can foster the spiritual journeys of members
plus organize to support each one's vision, call, and gifts, inquire
about the authors' "Recreating the Church" packet of articles:
1309 Merchant Lane, McLean, VA 22101.

As a follow-up to this course, some people have found value in
reading the Scriptures selected for the coming Sunday liturgy.
Typically, these include a selection from the Hebrew Scriptures,
the Psalms, the Epistles, and the Gospels. Many churches follow
an ecumenical lectionary shared by Roman Catholic and a num-

ber of Protestant denominations. By meditating on these readings, one joins the rhythm of the liturgical year and the many churches around the world using them.

These organizations have publications and programs that support and nourish our relationship with God.

Cursillo Movement. This Roman Catholic effort offers weekend retreats during which participants are exposed to a rich experience of God's love. There is then opportunity to join reunion groups whose purpose is to keep alive this experience of love and to encourage participants to carry this love to work, home, community, and church. Address: The Cursillo Movement, Center of the National Secretariat, 4500 West Davis Street, P.O. Box 210226, Dallas, TX 75211.

The National Episcopal Cursillo is sponsored by people in the Episcopalian tradition. Address: P.O. Box 213, Cedar Falls, IA 50613. Phone: (319) 266-5323.

The Upper Room Emmaus in Nashville offers a similar experience and is sponsored by Methodists. Address: 1908 Grand Ave., Box 189, Nashville, TN 37202-0189. Phone: (615) 340-7227.

International Young Life. P.O. Box 520, Colorado Springs, CO 80901. Phone: (719) 590-7733. An interdenominational youth movement that focuses on faith development in young people.

Women's Alliance for Theology, Ethics, and Ritual. 8035 13th Street, Silver Spring, MD 20910. Phone: (301) 589-2509. Offers programs and publications to help people nationally and internationally be part of an inclusive church and society.

Additional resources are listed in *Discovering Your Gifts, Vision, and Call.*

ACKNOWLEDGMENTS

Like all books, this one has a story behind it. Telling that story allows us to thank all the people who helped along the way and also gives you, the reader, some background on how this was written and why.

In a sense this book began when Lois Donnelly, a Catholic, joined with Jackie McMakin and Pat Davis, both Protestants, to offer workshops and courses in local churches. Jean Sweeney and Rhoda Nary, both Catholics, soon joined us. We took the name Partners because we experienced great creativity when as Catholics and Protestants we partnered together to do our work.

Some of us received training in experiential design from Faith at Work. We were inspired by the work of the Taizé Community in France, started by Roger Schutz, a Swiss Reformed pastor, who drew together Roman Catholic and Protestant men to live a monastic life dedicated to "a passion for unity."

Becoming dissatisfied with our "piecemeal" workshops and courses, we were ready for what became a life-changing question: "If you could do anything you wanted in churches, what would it be?"

We had been students at the Church of the Saviour's School of Christian Living and had been deeply affected by the courses offered there. Founded by Gordon and Mary Cosby its story has been chronicled by Elizabeth O'Connor. Could we design a similar set of courses that would present the treasures of both Catholic and Protestant traditions in a format that busy people could respond to?

What resulted were the four courses contained in the *Doorways* Series. When they were offered, several participants wanted to join us in the Partners Community: Susan Hogan, Cathie Bates, Dave Scheele, Mid Allen, Ricci Waters, Sally Dowling, Sancy Scheele, Coby Pieterman, and Charlotte Rogers. Each of these people added their ideas to the courses as we developed them further.

Participants then began to ask, "Could you give us the course materials so we could facilitate them ourselves and take them to other places?"

Jackie began to translate the notes and outlines into book form but soon got bogged down. Rhoda volunteered to help, and from then on we worked together, Jackie as writer, Rhoda as editor, both as conceptualizers. The Partners gave tremendous support throughout the process and helped a great deal with finishing touches. Others who helped were Mim Dinndorf, Sonya Dyer, Mary Elizabeth Hunt, Maggie Kalil, Gertrude Kramer, Billie Johansen, Mary Pockman, Janet Rife, Mary Scantlebury, and Gretchen Hannon. Our first editor was Cy Riley from Winston Press.

Liberation, black, creation, and feminist theologies have shown us how limited are our contemporary thought patterns and organizational structures. These theologies stress the Gospel's "preferential option for the poor," the importance of valuing and incorporating the experience of nonwhite, Third World, female, oppressed, and marginalized persons.

In such a theologically fertile period, when new understandings are being lived, shared, and written about at an amazing rate, each choice of word, phrase, or emphasis has theological implications. Whatever we write, in one sense, is quickly dated. Yet, in another sense, we are trying to capture and describe some of the timeless aspects of Christian faith. This book would serve a good purpose if our attempts to preserve the old and incorporate the new stimulated each of you to do this personally.

Since first published in 1984, the *Doorways* Series has found its way to several countries outside our own, most notably Mexico. There it has enjoyed wide use. A Spanish translation called *Puertas al Encuentro*, including Mexican examples, was created by Mari Carmen Mariscal and associates.[1] Several stories of our Mexican friends are included in this revision.

For this new edition, we are indebted to editor Kandace Hawkinson for seeing the possibility of a brand-new format—each course presented in a single book. She and her fellow editor, Ron Klug, have been wonderful to work with. Others here at home have been a big help, some for the second time: Millie Adams, Marjorie Bankson, Connie Francis, Lynn Parent, Ellen Radday, Gay Bland, Gretchen Hannon, Martha Hlavin, Mary Moore, and Valerie Vesser. Our husbands, Dave McMakin and Bill Nary, and our children, Tom and Peg McMakin and Brendan, Kristin, Kevin, and Paul Nary, have given lots of support, each in different ways.

We would like to hear from you about any reactions and suggestions you have that will help improve this approach to strengthening your spiritual life. If you would like us to partner with you as you consider next steps after using the *Doorways* Series, we are available for consultation, training, and retreats.

Jacqueline McMakin
1309 Merchant Lane
McLean, VA 22101
(703) 827–0336

Rhoda Nary
4820 N. 27th Place
Arlington, VA 22207
(703) 538–6132

NOTES

Introduction

1. Rosemary Radford Ruether, *Sexism and God-Talk* (Boston: Beacon Press, 1983), p. 116.

2. For an important discussion of these issues, see Tom F. Driver, *Christ in a Changing World* (New York: Crossroad Publishing Co., 1981).

3. Inclusive Language Lectionary Committee, *An Inclusive Language Lectionary* (Philadelphia: Westminster Press, 1983), Appendix.

Session 1

1. John Bright, *The Kingdom of God* (New York: Abingdon Press, 1953), p. 191.

2. Celia Hahn, "Keeping the Sabbath: A Conversation with Tilden Edwards," *Action Information* 7: (Nov.–Dec. 1981), p. 1.

3. Hahn, "Keeping the Sabbath," pp. 1, 2.

4. Quoted by Evelyn Underhill, *Light of Christ* (Wilton, CT: Morehouse-Barlow, 1982), p. 32.

5. Richard Rohr, "A Life Pure and Simple," *Sojourners*, vol. 10, no. 12 (Dec. 1981), p. 13.

Session 2

1. Judith Funderburk, *Healing the Whole Person: A Process-Oriented Expressive Arts Approach to Therapy*, unpublished Master

of Arts Thesis, pp. 199–200. Available from the author: 531 S. Harrison St., Arlington, VA 22204. Phone: (703) 671–5310.

2. Norman Cousins, *Anatomy of an Illness* (New York: W. W. Norton, 1979).

3. *Newsweek*, January 6, 1992. p. 40.

Session 3

1. Leslie Weatherhead, *The Transforming Friendship* (Nashville, TN: Abingdon, 1928), p. 28.

2. Weatherhead, *Transforming Friendship*, p. 60.

3. Ralph Keifer, "A Spirituality of Mystery," *Spirituality Today* 33 (June 1981): 107.

4. Keifer, "Spirituality of Mystery," p. 107.

5. Irene Claremont de Castillejo, *Knowing Woman* (New York: Harper & Row, 1973), p. 117.

6. Albert Nolan, *Jesus Before Christianity* (Maryknoll, NY: Orbis Books, 1978), p. 117.

7. Nolan, *Jesus Before Christianity*, p. 39.

8. Evelyn Underhill, *Light of Christ* (New York: David McKay Co., Inc., 1956), p. 27.

9. Ken Unger, "Healing a Broken Heart," *Faith at Work*, Sept.–Oct. 1991, p. 5.

10. Jean Houston, *Godseed* (Wheaton, IL: Theosophical Publishing, 1992), p. 13.

11. Houston, *Godseed*, p. 98.

12. Frank Laubach, *Letters by a Modern Mystic* (Syracuse, NY: New Readers Press, 1979), p. 46.

13. C. G. Jung, *Modern Man in Search of a Soul,* trans. Del and Baynes (London: Routledge and Kegan Paul, 1933), pp. 271–272.

Session 4

1. Henri J. M. Nouwen, *In the Name of Jesus* (New York: Crossroad Publishing, 1989), p. 26.

2. John McGuire, *The Dance of Life.* No further documentation known.

3. Rose Marciano Lucey, *Roots and Wings* (San Jose, CA: Resource Publications, 1987), pp. 38–39.

4. Dorothee Sölle, *Choosing Life* (Philadelphia: Fortress Press, 1981), p. 55.

5. Pierre Teilhard de Chardin, *The Divine Milieu* (New York: Harper & Row, 1960), p. 128.

6. Source unknown.

Session 5

1. Walter Brueggemann, *The Prophetic Imagination* (Philadelphia: Fortress Press, 1973), p. 97.

2. J. B. Phillips, *The Young Church in Action: A Translation of the Acts of the Apostles* (New York: Macmillan, 1955), p. viii.

3. John C. Haughey, *The Conspiracy of God: The Holy Spirit in Us* (Garden City, NY: Image Books, Doubleday, 1976), p. 44.

4. John Welch, *When Gods Die: An Introduction to John of the Cross* (New York: Paulist Press, 1990), p. 204.

5. Gerald G. May, *The Awakened Heart* (San Francisco: Harper-SanFrancisco, 1991), p. 80.

6. May, *Awakened Heart*, p. 83.

7. "Joseph Campbell's Spiritual Challenge" (taped address). Sounds True, 1825 Pearl St., Boulder, CO 80302.

Session 6

1. John Black, *Canberra Take Aways* (Geneva: WCC Publications, 1991).

2. John Haughey, *The Conspiracy of God* (Garden City, NY: Doubleday Image Books, 1976), p. 69.

3. Haughey, *Conspiracy of God*, p. 69.

4. George Fox, quoted by Thomas Kelly, *The Eternal Promise* (New York: Harper & Row, 1966), pp. 52–59.

5. Fox, *Eternal Promise*, p. 47.

6. The story of Roger Schutz and Taizé is told by Kathryn Spink in *A Universal Heart* (San Francisco: Harper & Row, 1986).

7. Sherry Ruth Anderson and Patricia Hopkins, *The Feminine Face of God: The Unfolding of the Sacred in Women* (New York: Ballantine Books, 1991), p. 99.

8. "To Avert a Common Danger," *Parade Magazine*, March 1, 1992, pp. 10ff.

Next Steps

1. Albert Nolan, *Jesus Before Christianity* (Maryknoll, NY: Orbis Book: 1978), p. 138.

2. John Welch, *When Gods Die* (New York: Paulist Press, 1990), p. 205.

3. This is one of the sayings of the Desert Fathers of the fourth Century in Thomas Merton, *The Wisdom of the Desert* (New York: New Directions, 1960), p. 50.

Acknowledgments

1. Available from Edamex, Heriberto Frias #1104, Mexico 03100, D. F. Mexico, or from the authors.